Rethinking China

Zhengyu Z. Huang

Rethinking China

Challenging Our Economic Assumptions & Opportunities for Lasting Prosperity

palgrave
macmillan

Zhengyu Z. Huang
Yu Capital
New York City, NY, USA

ISBN 978-981-95-3607-8 ISBN 978-981-95-3608-5 (eBook)
https://doi.org/10.1007/978-981-95-3608-5

Cover credit: seksan Mongkhonkhamsao

This Palgrave Macmillan imprint is published by the registered company Springer Nature Singapore Pte Ltd.
The registered company address is: 152 Beach Road, #21-01/04 Gateway East, Singapore 189721, Singapore

Contents

CHAPTER 1

Introduction

A few days into my tenure as President of the Committee of 100, in the waning year of the first Donald Trump administration, with COVID-19 lockdowns in effect throughout America, I logged on to a secure virtual meeting with senior officials from the State Department. "Mr. Huang, you represent an organization of the most prominent Chinese Americans in this country, as such, you must understand that the relationship between the United States and China has fundamentally changed," intoned one of the key officials in charge of implementing President Trump's China policies at the State Department. "We are divided by *Intellectual Property (IP) theft, unfair trade/economics, human rights violations, Taiwan*, and much more. This is an existential struggle between democracy and autocracy, our way of life and theirs. As Chinese Americans, you must take a stand."

I took a deep breath, feeling the immensity of his words and the historic nature of the shift. With the deterioration in relations between the United States and the People's Republic of China (PRC), I grasped that my community—the five million Chinese Americans living in America—was squarely caught in the middle. With President Trump and other politicians' irresponsible use of phrases such as "Kung-flu," and "China Virus," a total of 10,095 hate incidents against Asian American and Pacific Islander (AAPI) persons were reported to Stop AAPI Hate from March 19, 2020 to December 31, 2021 [1]. As many Americans cannot tell the

Z. Z. Huang, *Rethinking China*,
https://doi.org/10.1007/978-981-95-3608-5_1

difference between a Chinese or Korean or Filipino American, suddenly 20 million Asian Americans were in the crosshairs. In 2021, the New York Police Department (NYPD) reported a 361 percent increase in anti-Asian hate crimes [2]. In 2022, a Texas man attacked a Burmese American family in a Sam's Club and tried to kill the father and his 6-year-old son because he believed that they were Chinese and spreading the COVID-19 virus in America [3]. And I feared that it might only get worse. Beyond concern for my community, wonderment bubbled inside of me. What are the assumptions underlying this fundamental shift from engagement to existential struggle between the world's two largest and most consequential economies? For if the assumptions are true, this struggle would affect every American and every Chinese, and most likely touch every country in the world. This is a question that must be of concern to all free-thinking Americans.

First, a bit about me. I was born in Shanghai and came to the United States at the age of ten. My father was one of the first generation of Chinese students to come study in the US after the Chinese Cultural Revolution and Deng Xiaoping's opening up and reform program in the early 1980s. I grew up in Los Angeles, attended public schools and went to college at Stanford University where I received a B.S. in Industrial Engineering, a B.A. in Economics, and a M.S. in Computer Science. My first job out of college was with Intel Corporation, where I rose to become the youngest Managing Director at the time. Intel was kind enough to pay for my MBA at Harvard Business School and after graduation, sent me to China charged with negotiating with the PRC government on IP transfer and 4G collaborations, culminating in an agreement among Intel, the Ministry of Information and Industry, Huawei, ZTE and others. In 2009, I left Intel and served a year as a White House Fellow under President Barack Obama, working at the US Agency for International AID (USAID) as special assistant to the administrator. Afterwards I started a financial services data company headquartered in Shanghai, serving international and domestic institutional investors interested in the Chinese market. In 2014, I left China and returned to the US, soon founding an investment firm that focused on K12 education in the US. All the while, I wrote four books in Chinese, that sold over 300,000 copies in China. As a published author, I have visited over forty cities across China, met with Chinese from all walks of life, and conducted hundreds of online and offline talks in China that have garnered more than fifty million views.

In 2019, out of the blue I received a call from a headhunter. Are you interested in the role of President at the Committee of 100? The Committee of 100 was founded in 1990, when Henry Kissinger approached the noted architect I.M. Pei and asked whether Chinese Americans might contribute to the then burgeoning relationship between the US and PRC. I.M. Pei, famed cellist YoYo Ma, and a few others started the Committee of 100 as a nonprofit, membership-based organization of Americans of Chinese descent dedicated to a dual mission: Chinese American inclusion in America and a more productive US–China relationship. The membership has since grown to more than 130 members; notable members include Gary Locke, former governor of Washington State, former Commerce Secretary, and former Ambassador to China; Jerry Yang, founder of Yahoo!; Eric Yuan, founder of Zoom; David Ho, Time Magazine Man of the Year for his pioneering work on HIV/AIDS; and many others. Though I had little interaction with the Committee of 100 before then, I was motivated by one changing reality. For the first time, I didn't feel safe for my mom to take her daily walk around her Bay Area neighborhood alone. Stories abounded of elderly Asian women being punched in the face, pushed off the sidewalk, and much worse [4]. Although I felt like I could defend myself, the Committee of 100 seemed like one of the few notable organizations in our community, that could do more for all of us. The selection process took a while, but ultimately I was chosen, as I was told, because of my business and government leadership experiences, as well as my ability to traverse American and Chinese cultures.

At Harvard Business School, we learned the phrase GIGO (garbage in, garbage out), or garbage input, garbage output. In other words, if we operate under the wrong assumptions, even with the perfect model and unlimited resources, we are likely to obtain bad outcomes. This applies to business as well as government. America went to war in Iraq under the false assumption that Saddam Hussein harbored weapons of mass destruction. America went to war in Afghanistan under the false assumption that in order to defeat Al Qaeda, we must first defeat the Taliban. Trillions of dollars spent, tens of thousands of American lives lost, and decades later, we are hard pressed to say that Iraq, Afghanistan, their respective regions, or our American homeland are made safer because of those wars. If America is to engage in an existential struggle with the PRC, a country with many times the economic and military capacity of Iraq or Afghanistan, a country with nuclear weapons that can reach our homeland, we must ascertain that our assumptions are, as much as the data and evidence would allow, correct. Repeating the errors of Iraq or Afghanistan, in our contest with the PRC, would be catastrophic for American security at home and interests abroad.

When I was a White House Fellow, I had the opportunity to meet with former Secretary of State Colin Powell and former Secretary of Defense Donald Rumsfeld. Powell was open in admitting that had he the opportunity to do things again, he would not have said what he said, in the runup to the 2003 Iraq War. Rumsfeld on the other hand, repeated that he operated with the best assumptions he had at the time. Today, archival evidence undeniably illustrates that Powell had tremendous misgivings on the validity and applicability of the evidence before his now infamous UN speech, and Rumsfeld actively suppressed alternative data sources and viewpoints that did not accord with his assumptions. I believe that the many public servants whom I have encountered truly believe in their mission to protect American values and serve American interests, but I also believe, to borrow President Ronald Reagan's words, we Americans have the obligation to trust and verify what our government tells us. Not just because our government works for us, the American taxpayers, but because we bear the consequences.

So, trust and verify I did. In the more than 3 years as President of the Committee of 100, I spoke to and met with hundreds of US–China experts, including leading academics from Harvard, Yale, Stanford, Oxford, Cambridge, and many other American and European universities, as well as well-known thought leaders from think tanks such as the Center for Strategic and International Studies (CSIS), Brookings Institution, Hoover Institution, American Enterprise Institute, and many others. I spoke with most of the former US Ambassadors to China, as well as representatives of leading American firms based in China. I leaned on the membership of the Committee of 100, many of whom have extensive experiences serving in the US government, acting as CEOs of American firms in China, starting significant businesses in China, or engaging in cultural exchanges between the US and China. Most importantly, I worked closely with the White House, the State Department, the Department of Justice, the FBI, and dozens of congressional offices in the House and Senate at the intersection of national security and civil liberties.

What I found astounded me. Most of the assumptions under which America is operating with regard to the PRC are overblown or misleading. A good number are patently false. Time and again I repeated what I heard from our government to experts, and time and again I was presented with data that contradicted those assumptions. Where data wasn't available, I was able to collaborate with academic institutions to conduct independent research. For example, when President Trump pronounces that the PRC steals $600 billion of IP annually from the US, how does he arrive at the number? When the FBI director asserts that IP theft from the PRC is state sponsored and that it is a whole of society attack, how do surveys of economic espionage cases bear out his claim? When presidential candidates concur that China is the cause of American job loss, what does the data and evidence say? When the State Department argues that China is laying debt traps around the world, what does the longest tracking database on Chinese overseas investments say? When over and over again political leaders point to America's vital role in defending the international rules-based system, what is our government doing in reality? When our military leaders tell us that military deterrence is the solution to preventing war in Taiwan and that defending Taiwan is defending democracy, what might be the consequences of those martial words?

What I hope to do in this book is to present you, the reader, with the data and evidence that I have gathered, so that you may form your own informed opinions. I will first present you with the prevalent assumptions, and the data and evidence that support those assumptions. I will then present you additional data and evidence, that you may not have seen or heard of, but that are credible and oftentimes comprised of decades of research and data gathered by noted American institutions. It is true, that when it comes to US–China relations, data is not always available. For example, the US media has widely reported on de-coupling of American firms from China. Yet, supply chain data, on a firm level, is considered extremely proprietary, and thus difficult to collate. I am fortunate that with the platform afforded by the Committee of 100 and through my personal networks I could gather on the ground stories and insights. I will share these with you because they oftentimes diverge from the pronouncements of our government or media.

What this book is not about is presenting the Chinese side or the Chinese story. Neither I nor any American can truly tell you how President Xi Jinping really thinks or what his designs for the world are. What I am able to do is present you with all the data, evidence, and stories that will help you make better informed assumptions with regard to our situation with the PRC. I have struggled mightily in deciding whether I should proffer alternative courses of action, but knowing that the intelligent reader will ask, "if assumption x is wrong, and assumption y is more likely based on the data, then what courses of action may we draw from the updated assumption?" I have thus offered my suggested assumptions and courses of action. But the reader needs not agree with any of them.

In my many meetings in Washington D.C., I have been told repeatedly that Democrats and Republicans may not agree on anything else, but they agree on being tough on China. Yet privately I have also heard thoughtful leaders worry about the lack of intellectual rigor and debate on arguably the most important foreign policy matter of our times. I don't presume that a single book by an unheralded author will change the course of history. But I do hope that the data and evidence presented in this book will create a narrative space, so that honest debate and frank discourse can occur, and that we can make the best decisions using the most realistic and accurate assumptions. I have been advised to stay quiet, for surely I will be attacked as many Chinese Americans have already been attacked. Congresswoman Judy Chu from California, a long-time public servant, had her loyalties questioned by Representative Lance Gooden of Texas because she spoke up for another Chinese American who was falsely attacked [5]. The advice to me from many Chinese Americans is to keep my head down, stay quiet, and hope that the attention doesn't fall on me. The hysteria over China has gotten to such a fevered pitch that quite a few academics whom I have spoken to said that you are free to use my published research, but please don't quote me because I don't want the trouble. Anyone who questions the orthodox assumptions of today is simply branded as a panda hugger, pro-Beijing, or worse, agent or spy of the PRC. But as a naturalized citizen, I remember taking my oath of allegiance, and it stayed with me. I believe that it is my duty as an American citizen to speak up when things are not right, and that just as I expect my country to protect me, I must do my part to protect my country.

Yes, I have business, family, and cultural ties to China. But I believe that those ties make me a better investigator and analyst of the assumptions that undergird our current China policies. Chinese Americans, despite being in the US for more than 170 years, still labor under the century old stereotype of the perpetual foreigner, of harboring dual loyalties or worse. As I have said to news outlets repeatedly, Chinese Americans are not national security liabilities, we are national security assets [6]. We are patriotic Americans who are proud of our Chinese heritage, and we have unique and valuable insights to offer our country in managing the most important bilateral relationship of our times. A critic may disagree with some of the data offered in this book and retort, what about other data and evidence? I would welcome that as exactly the end I hope to achieve: a vigorous and thoughtful debate grounded in data and evidence, so that our policymakers can operate with the most realistic assumptions in charting our courses of action.

One obstacle to a robust discussion on US–China relations is the matter of classified information. In countless meetings, inside and outside the US government, I have heard the line, "the intelligence community has shared information with us that affirms these assumptions, which we are not at liberty to share with the public." As a White House Fellow, I had to go through an extensive security clearance process to receive top secret clearance, and I understand the importance of protecting our nation's secrets and their sources. However, evidence in real life does not accord with the alleged magnitude of the threat. For example, in 2018, Attorney General Jeff Sessions announced the China Initiative, to tackle a supposed state sponsored attempt by the PRC to steal IP from the US [7]. Three years later, the MIT Technology Review examined 77 cases and 150 defendants filed under the China Initiative and found that none of the cases had anything to do with economic espionage. Only 25% of the cases resulted in some form of conviction (with nothing to do with economic espionage) and 90% were targeted toward scientists of Chinese descent [8]. One cannot help but ask: if the intelligence is so spot on, if the theft is so widespread, why is it that we failed to convict anyone of economic espionage under the China Initiative, when the FBI director claimed that every 10 hours a PRC-related counterintelligence case is opened [9]? The US intelligence community garnered tremendous credibility when it released information detailing Russian plans to attack Ukraine before the Russian invasion. More openness and transparency on data would be much welcomed in the debate on US–China relations. A word that I've heard often used in Washington D.C. to stifle dissent is *naïve*. Anyone who voices a difference of opinion on the prevalent assumptions on China is simply accused of being naïve, of not understanding the existential threat that is the PRC: that not doing enough is the problem, not too much. I believe that we should let the data and evidence do the talking. True naivete is operating on fear rather than logic, on imagination rather than reality.

When I first explained the premise of the book to an entrepreneur friend he was visibly shaken and exclaimed, "are you saying that China is not a threat?" I believe that is not the right question to ask. The better question may be, "what kind of threat is China?" As my friend hails from a state that experiences hurricanes I ventured an analogy. If a category 5 hurricane comes your way you should jump into your car and get out of dodge. If a category 1 hurricane lands you would simply bring in your valuables and lock up your windows. Depending on the threat level, we respond accordingly and appropriately. Today unfortunately, with the hysteria over China, every action is deemed a category 6 hurricane, and thus our responses become unmeasured and oftentimes against our own interests.

From time to time, I will introduce alternative frames of reference for the reader to consider. I have learned a few during my interactions with various experts that have significantly expanded my mindset on what is possible, versus what we stand to lose. For example, a frequent comment I hear in discussing US–China relations is that China is a rising power challenging the international rules-based systems that the US established, through blood and iron, in particular in the Pacific. That framing suggests that either the rising power or the established power must give way, and that there will be a winner and a loser. Yet a cursory study of history shows that China's pre-eminence in Southeast and East Asia dates back more than one thousand years, so much so that countries such as Korea, Japan, and Vietnam adopted its language, culture, and political systems. So much so that in the 1400s, Admiral Zheng He commanded the largest naval fleet in the world and captained seven voyages comprised of 300 ships that went as far as Africa. Today's China should be properly labeled as a resurgent power. The US, though dominant in Asia since the end of World War II, in the larger context of history, is better recognized as an upstart power. For an upstart power and a resurgent power there is no pre-defined end state. Such a frame of reference may provide participants with more options for possible win–win equilibrium.

Several D.C. insiders have asked me, for whom is the book intended? For they believe, rightfully, that elected officials in Washington D.C. will be hard pressed, for political reasons, to appear soft on China. That no matter what the data and evidence offered, our courses of action are set. Perhaps they are correct. Perhaps all I can hope for is that there will be enough light created that one or two policymakers may say, wait a second, can we sit down and revisit our assumptions before we move ahead with our proposed courses of action? Perhaps that is enough to create space for debate and discourse. A retired Senator told me that my attempts may be futile. He believes that politicians are motivated by elections, and that the American public doesn't care about foreign policy. In fact, in his observation of history, the American public will willingly follow our political leaders into a foreign war and only raise questions 6 months later. Perhaps he is correct. But in my travels across the US, I have found many thoughtful Americans who care passionately and deeply about climate change, artificial intelligence, nuclear nonproliferation, and preventing the next global pandemic. None of these global issues that affect every American, can be solved without collaborations between the US and PRC. Sam Altman, CEO of OpenAI, called for collaborations with China to counter the risk of artificial intelligence [10], because he and any thoughtful American know that we cannot tackle the world's greatest challenges, without the world's two most powerful economies participating.

In my recent visits to Washington D.C., the talk has moved on from being tough on China to openly preparing for war. Make no mistake, I believe that we are engaged in war with the PRC today. We are engaged in a technology war, a trade war, a currency war, a war of words, and if some pundits are correct, a proxy war over Ukraine. The only war we are not engaged in today but dangerously close to is an armed conflict. In all my conversations with experts on this topic, none has been able to present a scenario in which an open armed conflict between the US and PRC does not involve immense bloodshed on both sides, and does not present the potential for catastrophic suffering on both sides. In my meeting with the group Veterans for Peace, I came away with the feeling that these veterans, who fought in America's wars, were not simply traumatized by the horrors of war, but by the futility of wars without clear ends and metrics for success. Meetings after meetings I had asked a simple question, "if we were to go to war with the PRC, what would long-term, durable success look like?" and time and time again I received muddled, incomprehensible answers. If we are to prepare for an armed conflict with the PRC, then we must be crystal clear what our end goals and metrics for success are, so that the failures of Iraq and Afghanistan are not repeated. I believe that all Americans care about this because the trillions of dollars that may be spent can otherwise be spent on job creation, infrastructure, and our people at home. This book is thus intended for all free-thinking Americans who care enough to pick up a book on foreign policy, because I hope you will discover, as I have, that the assumptions have more to do with domestic policies than foreign, and that the courses of action emanating from these assumptions will affect every one of us, like it or not.

Words matter. And the words of our political leaders matter a lot. That is why at the Committee of 100, I worked with leading experts in Asian American studies, political science, statecraft and diplomacy, and media and communications to craft our anti-Asian hate glossary [11] and our US–China diplomatic language guide [12]. The Anti-Asian hate glossary and the US–China diplomatic language guide have been shared with and used by the White House, the State Department, the Congressional Asian Pacific American Caucus (CAPAC), among other federal and local agencies. Americans understand instinctively the distinctions among the American people, their elected government for the present 4 years, and a particular political party. Similarly, in speaking about US–China we must clearly differentiate between China the historical, cultural, and geographical entity, the Chinese people, the PRC government in power, and Americans of Chinese descent. In this book, as much as possible, I will use PRC to refer to the government in China, and its policies and positions. I will sometimes use China because it was used by the speaker, and I want to preserve as much as possible the original words said. Chinese Americans refer to the five million or so American citizens of Chinese descent or green card holders on the pathway to citizenship. I understand that recently it's become fashionable to ascribe the existential struggle between the US and China to one between the US and the Chinese Communist Party (CCP). Of course we are engaged in an existential struggle with China, how can we not as a liberal democracy against a Communist Party? It is certainly true that under President Xi, the difference between the PRC government and the CCP is becoming narrower, and most, not all, PRC government officials are CCP members. Margaret Lewis, Professor of Law at Seton Hall, uses the term party-state to define the one-party rule in China with the CCP as the sole ruling party. Yet I cannot find any evidence that China is actively promoting Communist ideologies abroad, and with the private sector contributing 60% of GDP at home, China can hardly be described as a textbook case for Communism. As much as I can, I will refrain from using CCP because it easily conjures up the false comparison to the Cold War between the US and the Soviet Union. All experts I've spoken to agree that what we face today between the US and PRC is fundamentally different from what the US and Soviet Union faced, then framed as an existential struggle between democracy and Communism. There will be a Cold War if we really want it, but we should think long and hard, test out our assumptions thoroughly, before we embark on another fifty years of life and death Cold War struggle.

I want to be explicit in stating that the viewpoints and opinions espoused in this book are mine and mine alone. Yes, they are buttressed by noted and credible experts who have spent their lives researching in their particular fields, but the conclusions are mine alone. They do not represent the opinions of the Committee of 100 nor of any of its members. The Committee of 100, despite its membership being all Americans, has been attacked in the media for being sympathetic to or under the influence of the PRC [13]. As I'll explain more in a subsequent chapter, these types of attacks will only intensify with the worsening of relations, and this is one of the principal reasons that I write this book only after leaving the Committee of 100. I write from the Chinese American perspective. Chinese Americans today contribute extensively to the US economy, their involvement spanning small businesses in essential services such as food and laundry, and technical professions including medicine, education, and engineering. In 2019, they contributed over $300 billion to US GDP through consumer spending, supporting 3 million jobs. There are over 160,000 Chinese American owned businesses, generating approximately $240 billion in revenue and supporting 1.3 million jobs as of 2017. Fortune 500 companies founded by Chinese Americans have supported hundreds of thousands of jobs, and their market capitalization has reached as high as $4 trillion. Chinese Americans have also come to play a greater role in public and institutional life. As their political rights have strengthened, Chinese Americans have played a more active role in civil service and political activities. Between 2009 and 2018, Chinese Americans' employment in public administration grew by 68%, outpacing the growth of the Chinese American population and of the public administration workforce as a whole. Chinese Americans have played an important and underreported role in American national defense, from military enrollment to scientific and professional contributions to defense and security agencies. One out of every five Chinese American men served in the US Armed Forces in World War II, many earning decorations for bravery. As outer space becomes a geopolitical hotspot, one in 25 aerospace engineers is Chinese American [14].

The Chinese American community is extremely diverse. We are descendants of laborers who came here to build the transatlantic railroads in the mid-1800s, as well as more recent immigrants from mainland China, Taiwan, Hong Kong, and the larger Chinese diaspora worldwide. We oftentimes disagree more than we agree. In 2022, working with Columbia University and more than one hundred Chinese American community organizations nationwide, the Committee of 100 conducted the largest and most in-depth survey of our community ever [15]. Roughly three out of four Chinese Americans have reported some form of racial discrimination in the past 12 months. Despite that, the majority of Chinese Americans feel in tune with their American identity and want a more productive US–China relationship.

In high school European History class, we read about the Eighty Years War, great power rivalry between Spain and a rising Netherlands. We also studied the Hundred Years War, between the two great powers of the day, the English and the French, as they vied for global supremacy. If history is of any precedent, the great power rivalry between the US and PRC will likely take decades, if not centuries to play out. If this is indeed so, then there is added urgency and necessity that we get our assumptions right from the get-go, so that we make the best decisions for our people and our interests globally. As the subsequent pages illustrate, there is already strong evidence that the hysteria over China is hurting our values and competitiveness and ushering us on the path to war: whether in racial profiling of Chinese American scientists, cessation of international economic and scientific collaborations, withdrawal of American leadership from international rules-based systems, or military buildup without clear outcomes. Amidst the hysteria over China, this book hopes to explore the underlying assumptions that may better guide our courses of action. Left unaltered or unconsidered, they will ultimately leave us less competitive and less protected.

In my 3 years working on defending the rights of Chinese American scientists and combating anti-Asian hate and violence, I have come across numerous cases of bad actors trying to do harm to our country. When asked by the media about this or that case, my reply is always that, following due process, criminals and wrongdoers should be prosecuted to the fullest extent of the law. But American justice is about judging each case based on the merits of the case, and never guilt by association. Though the work has been grueling and the hours long, I have found a deeper faith in the American experiment. I have traveled to more than ninety countries and lived in five, yet nowhere have I found a country where a citizen can openly disagree with his government, and when he is right, though it takes time and effort, his government listens. I remember my head nodding in unison when in one of the State Department meetings a senior official said, "America isn't perfect, but we always try to do better." It is with that deep and unabating faith in our American values that I write.

Let us begin.

References

1. Stop AAPI Hate (2022) Stop AAPI Hate national report. Available at: https://stopaapihate.org/wp-content/uploads/2022/03/22-SAH-NationalReport-3.1.22-v9.pdf. Accessed 12 Aug 2025
2. NBC News (2021) NYPD reports 361 percent increase in anti-Asian hate crimes last year. Available at: https://www.nbcnews.com/news/asian-america/nypd-reports-361-percent-increase-anti-asian-hate-crimes-last-year-rcna8427. Accessed 12 Aug 2025
3. U.S. Department of Justice (2021) Texas man sentenced on hate crime charges for attacking Asian family. Available at: https://www.justice.gov/opa/pr/texas-man-sentenced-hate-crime-charges-attacking-asian-family. Accessed 12 Aug 2025
4. National Center for Biotechnology Information (2022) Asian American elders: caught in the crosshairs of a syndemic of racism, misogyny, and ageism during Coronavirus disease 2019. Available at: https://pmc.ncbi.nlm.nih.gov/articles/PMC9384670/. Accessed 12 Aug 2025
5. The Hill (2023) Texas Republican doubles down on attack on Judy Chu. Available at: https://thehill.com/homenews/house/3875852-texas-republican-doubles-down-on-attack-on-judy-chus-heritage/. Accessed 12 Aug 2025
6. CNN Business (2023) Asian Americans are anxious about hate crimes. TikTok ban rhetoric isn't helping. Available at: https://edition.cnn.com/2023/03/26/tech/asian-americans-tiktok/index.html. Accessed 12 Aug 2025
7. U.S. Department of Justice (2018) Attorney General Jeff Sessions announces new initiative to combat Chinese economic espionage. Available at: https://www.justice.gov/opa/speech/attorney-general-jeff-sessions-announces-new-initiative-combat-chinese-economic-espionage. Accessed 12 Aug 2025
8. MIT Technology Review (2021) The US crackdown on Chinese economic espionage is a mess. We have the data to show it. Available at: https://www.technologyreview.com/2021/12/02/1040656/china-initative-us-justice-department/. Accessed 12 Aug 2025

9. U.S. Department of Justice (2020) The China Initiative: Year-in-review 2019–20. Available at: https://www.justice.gov/opa/pr/china-initiative-year-review-2019-20. Accessed 12 Aug 2025
10. The Wall Street Journal (2023) OpenAI CEO calls for collaboration with China to counter AI risks. Available at: https://www.wsj.com/articles/openai-ceo-calls-for-collaboration-with-china-to-counter-ai-risks-eda903fe. Accessed 12 Aug 2025
11. Committee of 100 (2022) Anti-hate glossary. Available at: https://www.committee100.org/initiatives/anti-hate-glossary/. Accessed 12 Aug 2025
12. Committee of 100 (2023) U.S.–China language guide. Available at: https://www.committee100.org/wp-content/uploads/2023/02/Committee-of-100-US-China-Language-Guide-Feb-2023.pdf. Accessed 12 Aug 2025
13. Newsweek (2020) Exclusive: 600 U.S. groups linked to Chinese Communist Party influence effort with ambition beyond election. Available at: https://www.newsweek.com/2020/11/13/exclusive-600-us-groups-linked-chinese-communist-party-influence-effort-ambition-beyond-1541624.html. Accessed 12 Aug 2025
14. Committee of 100 (2023) Thematic report on Chinese American contributions: science and technology. Available at: https://www.committee100.org/wp-content/uploads/2023/09/Committee100-ThematicReport-ScienceAndTechnology.pdf. Accessed 12 Aug 2025
15. Committee of 100 (2022) The State of Chinese Americans survey 2022. Available at: https://www.committee100.org/state-of-chinese-americans-survey-webpage/. Accessed 12 Aug 2025

CHAPTER 2

Lessons from Vietnam and the Cold War

Time and again, as I listened to senior US government officials, I could not but draw a direct parallel between what is happening today with US–China relations and the series of decisions that led to the Vietnam War and their still searing consequences for America. From covert support of French military activities in Vietnam starting in the 1950s, to America's pulling out of South Vietnam in 1973 and South Vietnam's eventual downfall in 1975, the Vietnam War absorbed American attention and resources anywhere between 20 and 25 years. It spanned President Truman, Eisenhower, Kennedy, Johnson, and Nixon, and counted both Republicans and Democrats. In the end, over 58,000 US military personnel were killed, and more than 150,000 wounded. The US spent approximately $168 billion (equivalent to over $1 trillion in 2024 dollars) directly on the war. At home, the war contributed to significant inflation and increased national debt and diverted resources from domestic programs and infrastructure. President Johnson's signature program to combat poverty and inequality here in America—the Great Society—never got the funding it deserved due to the war. The Vietnam War led to widespread protests and deep division within American society. It led to a significant loss of trust in our government, especially after the release of the Pentagon Papers. So how did the best and the brightest of our government lead us astray? What can we learn from that conflict that inform how we may manage US–China relations today?

Z. Z. Huang, *Rethinking China*,
https://doi.org/10.1007/978-981-95-3608-5_2

1945 was a time when the problems of Europe were pre-eminent, when the question of the atomic weapon and the atomic balance with the Soviet Union was predominant, when even China was on the periphery, Vietnam was on the periphery of the periphery. But our entanglement in Vietnam began as early as July 1945, when the new and uncertain President of the United States, Harry Truman, made his first major trip abroad, to Potsdam. A decision was made at Potsdam on Vietnam, without any real consultation with experts. It concerned the surrender; the British would accept the Japanese surrender below the 16th parallel, the Chinese above it. Having accepted the surrender, the British would permit the French to return, and all subsequent events would flow from this: the French would reassert their authority, they would smile politely at all American requests to deal with the local population, but they would pay no attention; the French Indochina war would begin, and the Vietnamese would gain their freedom by force of arms [1].

At the very start, against the advice of and evidence presented by seasoned state department personnel, American political leaders believed that the battle between the French and the Vietnamese was one between democracy and Communism, instead of one between Colonialism and Nationalism. This assumption, which morphed into the domino theory—hypothesizing that if Vietnam falls, so too will other non-Communist countries in Asia—fundamentally blinded American leadership to the fact that while Communist, North Vietnam's fight was largely one for national independence and sovereignty. When Americans inherited the French position in Vietnam, we ignored unmistakable evidence that for all our worry about Vietnam's fall spreading to the rest of Asia, the potentially affected countries in Asia were not all that concerned. Eerily, today many American political leaders speak of the struggle between the US and PRC as one between democracy and autocracy, instead of one between a US-dominated world order and a more multipolar world order. The former assumption is black and white, and perhaps presages a struggle to the death. The latter assumption portends fierce competition, but also cooperation and compromises. In our protestations against Chinese transgressions worldwide, we seem to neglect the undeniable fact that almost all the potentially affected countries seem to welcome engagement with both the US and China, and are loathe to choose sides.

The Vietnam War occurred in the context of the Great Power struggle between the US and Soviet Union. Two great and uncertain powers were coming to terms with each other, a task made more difficult by their ideological differences (each believed its own myth about itself and its adversary) and by the additional frightening factor of the atomic weapon. Each thought its own policies basically defensive, and the policies of its adversary basically aggressive. A kind of demonology about a vast part of the world would become enshrined as accepted gospel. At home in America, one major political party (Democrats) would be too frightened to challenge it, the other (Republicans) delighted to reap the benefits from it [1]. And so too today we see both US and China each thinking its own policies basically defensive, and the policies of the other basically aggressive. The US is cementing new partnerships and alliances and increasing its military expenditures in response to Chinese aggressions and increased military expenditures; while the Chinese claim the exact same rationale for its escalating maneuvers abroad and military expenditures at home. Both countries have made national security the guiding light, willingly sacrificing economic, scientific, and technological cooperation and mutual benefits in order to protect themselves from the other. Political scientists speak of "security dilemmas": situations in which one state acts to make itself safer, but in doing so diminishes the security of other states, which in turn try to repair the damage through measures that diminish the security of the first state. The result is an ever-deepening whirlpool of distrust from which even the best-intentioned and most far-sighted leaders find it difficult to extricate themselves: their suspicions become self-reinforcing [2].

In private, the Kennedy administration mocked the bombast and rigidity of the Eisenhower years. Yet they did not reverse existing policies in Southeast Asia, a primary reason being that McCarthyism still lingered. McCarthyism went deeper in the American grain than most people wanted to admit. The Democrats, in the wake of the relentless sustained attacks on Truman over his policies in Asia, came to believe that they had lost the White House when China fell to the Communists in 1949. Long after McCarthy himself was gone, the fear of being accused of being soft on Communism lingered among Democratic leaders. The Republicans had, of course, offered no alternative policy on China and indeed there was no policy to offer, for China was never ours, and events there were well outside our control [1]. John Davies, a noted China expert in the State Department who was purged during the days of McCarthyism, never had any particular illusions about China, about how good and pro-American the Nationalists were or how evil the Communists were; he saw them both as being primarily Chinese, seeking China's special destiny; more Chinese than foreigners knew, more Chinese, perhaps, than they knew themselves. The United States, he believed, should let events take their own course (if only because there was no alternative; in China you could not control events, and if you tried, you were sucked into something monumentally futile). If anything, America should try and encourage independence for Communist China from Moscow, and above all, not push Mao into Stalin's hands [1].

Again and again, I hear the refrain that China was supposed to become more democratic as its economy liberalized; based on the belief that as more Chinese drank Starbucks and ate McDonalds, they were destined to become more American in political outlook as well. Yet as John Davies observed more than seventy years ago, China will likely seek its special destiny, bounded by its own constraints and aspirations. The new Red Scare today has made engagement with China all but impossible, and as much as we are loathe to admit, America has done our part to bind China and Russia closer together, not to mention Iran and North Korea. This is critical to note because the Vietnam War did not happen in a vacuum, but rather in the context of America mourning the "loss" of China, leading to its fear of losing more countries in Asia; and lingering McCarthyism, which made engagement and diplomacy in Vietnam all but impossible. In Vietnam we escalated in war making, but made little headways in diplomacy and dialog, always hoping for the other guy to feel the hurt first and come to the negotiations table. Yet the North Vietnamese matched our escalation in military buildup with their escalation in military buildup, our escalation in economic output for war with their escalation in economic output for war. It is not difficult to see the parallel to today, when China is matching our escalation in military buildup with their escalation in military buildup, our escalation in economic self-sufficiency with their escalation in economic self-sufficiency. President Nixon engaged China more than fifty years ago because he wanted to draw China away from Russia and reshape the Cold War. Through carrots and sticks, America should try and encourage independence for Beijing from Moscow, and above all, not to bind Russia, China, Iran, and North Korea into a formidable alliance. Yet with our own rhetoric, we attack ourselves for pursuing any path that may appear soft on the Chinese Communist Party.

In Vietnam, American political leaders believed that they had options, that whatever they had committed to, they could always pull back and pursue other options. The intervening years showed that time diminished options. As time progressed, the North Vietnamese would be that much stronger, the government in Saigon that much weaker, and the United States, having used force in Tonkin, that much more committed. When American political leaders came to make the final fateful decisions to put American combat troops on the ground, there would be options, but the real ones would be long since lost; the options they were dealing with were artificial ones. Given their outlook and their conception of the country and of their own political futures, they would be driven to certain inevitable, highly predictable decisions, but they still had the illusion that they could control events. If someone in those days had called them aside and suggested that they, all good rational men, were tied to a policy of deep irrationality, layer and layer of clear rationality based upon several great false assumptions and buttressed by a deeply dishonest reporting system which created a totally false data bank, they would have lashed out sharply that they did indeed know where they were going. Yet they forget, events are in the saddle and tend to ride mankind [1].

Early on, seasoned experts across the US government concluded that South Vietnam lacked popular support and could not fight the Viet Cong on its own. Barreling down the path that America did at the time, it was inevitable that American combat troops had to engage directly to prop up a failing regime. Yet data was hidden or distorted, experts were removed from positions and stations, and an active campaign was initiated by the executive branch to hide the truth from Congress, the media, and the American people. American political leaders clung fast to the assumption that with just a bit more bombing, just a bit more economic pressure, just a bit more on the ground support, our ally can stand on its own. Today, as will be more fully discussed in the chapter on Taiwan, Americans are told that with just a bit more military buildup, just a bit more economic pressure, just a bit more alliance building, China can be held at bay. Yet all experts I have spoken to agree that if an armed conflict develops in Taiwan, the only way Taiwan can remain independent is with direct US military intervention, leading to significant losses in American lives and equipment, with the real possibility of a prolonged and devastating war. Just as during the Vietnam War, events are in the saddle and tend to ride mankind. Supply chains de-coupled, economic sanctions and tariffs enacted, diplomacy stunted, militaries built up, and alliances guaranteed, if President Lai Ching Te of Taiwan, who is vocal in his support for Taiwanese independence, makes a sudden move, our options to not intervene militarily are limited to non-existent. Now just as during the Vietnam War, with the hysteria of the new Red Scare and our political leaders' conception of the country and of their own political futures, they would be driven to certain inevitable, highly predictable decisions. But they would still have the illusion that they could control events.

The United States triumphed in the Cold War. The Soviet Union fell. Yet hard lessons learned about avoiding nuclear Armageddon seem to be forgotten today. Wars had been fought as far back as anyone could remember. They accompanied the first tribes and settlements, and they persisted through the creation of cities, nations, empires, and modern states. They varied only in the means available with which to fight them: as technology advanced so too did lethality, with the unsurprising result that as wars became bigger, their costs became greater. This grim trend led the Prussian strategist Carl von Clausewitz, writing in the aftermath of the Napoleonic wars, to warn that states resorting to unlimited violence could be consumed by it. That is what Clausewitz meant when he insisted that war is "a continuation of political activity by other means... The political object is the goal, war is the means of reaching it, and means can never be considered in isolation from their purposes [2]."

The atomic bomb realized Clausewitz's vision of total and therefore purposeless war. BRAVO, an American nuclear test conducted in the Pacific on March 1, 1954, yielded 750 times the size of the Hiroshima bomb. The blast spread radioactive fallout hundreds of miles downwind, contaminating a Japanese fishing boat and killing a member of its crew. Less dangerous debris set off radiation detectors around the world. The question posed for nuclear warfighting was a stark one: if a single thermonuclear blast could have global ecological consequences, what would be the effects of using tens, hundreds, or thousands of nuclear weapons? "Atomic war will destroy civilizations," President Eisenhower insisted several months after the BRAVO test, "There will be millions of people dead... If the Kremlin and Washington ever lock up in a war, the results are too horrible to contemplate... But what kind of a contest would it be when the outlook comes close to destruction of the enemy and suicide for ourselves?" Winston Churchill, once again British prime minister, had only a few years earlier encouraged the Americans to provoke a military confrontation with the Soviet Union while their atomic monopoly remained in place. But now, in the aftermath of BRAVO, he completely reversed this position, pointing out to his wartime ally Eisenhower that only a few such explosions on British soil would leave his country uninhabitable [2].

It took the Cuban missile crisis of 1962 to finally persuade everyone involved that the weapons each side had developed during the Cold War posed a greater threat than the United States and the Soviet Union did to one another. The crisis, universally regarded now as the closest the world came to a third world war, provided a glimpse of a future no one wanted: of a conflict projected beyond restraint, reason, and the likelihood of survival. In the aftermath of the crisis, Secretary of Defense Robert McNamara repudiated his earlier idea of targeting only military facilities: instead, each side should target the other's cities, with the view to causing the maximum number of casualties possible. The new strategy became known as "Mutual Assured Destruction"—its acronym, MAD. The assumption behind it was that if no one could be sure of surviving a nuclear war, there would not be one. There was also the realization that the time had come, if not for the international control of nuclear weapons, then at least for agreements on how to manage them. The first of these came in 1963 with the Limited Test Ban Treaty, which abolished nuclear tests in the atmosphere. There followed, in 1968, the Nuclear Non-Proliferation Treaty, requiring nations possessing nuclear weapons not to help other states acquire them. And in 1972, the Strategic Arms Limitation Interim Agreement restricted the number of land—and sea-based ballistic missiles to be allowed to each side—with verification of compliance to take place by means of reconnaissance satellites. The Soviet Union and the United States also signed, in 1972, an Anti-Ballistic Missile Treaty that banned defenses against long-range missiles. The Cold War taught states to see—even in the absence of a common language, ideology, or set of interests—that they shared a stake in each other's survival, given the tiger themselves had created but now had to learn to live with [2].

Today, The United States is on track to spend the equivalent of more than two Manhattan projects per year in one of the most expensive nuclear arms races in history. As it stands now, this nuclear modernization comes with a price tag of approximately $1.7 trillion over 30 years. Since the launch of the modernization plan, every single nuclear-armed nation has begun redeveloping or expanding their nuclear arsenals. While some experts may argue what the specific cause of this may be, the US decision to spend nearly two trillion dollars on recapitalizing its nuclear arsenal was a significant factor. The PRC is adding hundreds of nuclear weapons to its arsenal after decades of maintaining a minimum deterrent posture of approximately 250 nuclear warheads. This response has only been further encouraged by continued US missile defense policies following President George W. Bush administration's withdrawal from the Anti-Ballistic Missile Treaty in 2002. Efforts to create new arms control agreements have been jettisoned as all parties increase spending in both the nuclear modernization and missile defense realms [3].

To stave off direct NATO military intervention in Ukraine, President Putin has made repeated veiled threats of tactical nuclear weapons deployment in an otherwise conventional war. But Russia is not alone in believing that nuclear weapons can be deployed in a conventional war. The United States is in the process of developing, producing, or deploying at least three new weapons systems that can be alternatively called: less-than-deterrent, non-strategic, tactical, or battlefield nuclear weapons. These classes of weapons are incredibly dangerous considering they are viewed as being smaller and less destructive and therefore more usable. Moreover, they are designed to be deployed alongside conventional forces, and their mere possession can be seen as increasing the likelihood of usage under pressure or in crisis situations. They also pose a significant discrimination problem for adversaries, by building uncertainty into American missile launches, forcing them to constantly evaluate if they are under a conventional or nuclear strike [3]. The Cold War taught all sides that the threat of nuclear annihilation can only be mitigated by forswearing nuclear weapons except as a final resort, and that nonproliferation and mutual verification work. Experts that I had spoken to universally assume that when it comes to a potential armed conflict around Taiwan, it will be a limited war, a conventional war, and a war that the US will win based on naval and air superiority alone. Yet the Cold War was clear in its lessons: nuclear armed countries must work together to ensure nonproliferation, nuclear armed countries must avoid direct armed conflict given the uncontrolled nature of military escalation, and nuclear arms agreements are in the interests of all parties. As much as one may argue that the escalation in the nuclear arms race today is egged on by the activities of others, the cold war taught us that America has a leading role and vital interest to ensure a world free of the threat of nuclear Armageddon.

The Soviet Union fell because by the 1980s its economy had stagnated, that despite its propaganda the standards of living of its citizens had fallen dreadfully behind. It simply was not able to keep the promises that it had made to its citizens, or to its Eastern European allies, either politically or economically. One hint of this came as early as March 1970, when the East German authorities invited West German Chancellor Brandt to visit

Erfurt [2]. To their intense embarrassment, hundreds of East Germans gathered under the hotel window to cheer their visitor. The contrast became so stark that when John Paul II kissed the ground at the Warsaw airport on June 2, 1979, he began the process by which communism in Poland—and ultimately everywhere else in Europe—would come to an end. Hundreds of thousands of his countrymen cheered his entry into the city. A million greeted him the next day in Gniezno. By the time the pope reached his home city of Krakow, between 2 and 3 million people were there to welcome him [2]. The 1960s and 1970s were not easy times for the United States, the Vietnam War, followed by economic stagflation, cast significant doubts in the trustworthiness of the US government and its economic policies. Yet despite the shock of Watergate and the disclosure of presidential criminal actions, the constitution of the United States prevailed. The contrast was stark, in the US, no one is above the law, and the economy, driven by innovation and entrepreneurship, is capable of weathering crises and setbacks. The US triumphed in the Cold War because its system proved to be better.

In the 1980s to 2000s, whenever I visited China and people found out that I traveled from the US, almost all spoke admiringly of the freedoms and standard of living enjoyed by Americans. Yet more recently, more questions arise where before words of admiration filled: why is the US prone to dramatic economic upheavals? Why is politics in America so divisive? Why is public safety in America so dismal? Why is America a better model to ensure that the fruits of economic progress reach all spectra of society? Just as in the Cold War, whichever model that addresses these existential questions of our times will win the hearts and minds of people everywhere, including here in America. As Gorbachev had told President George W. Bush at Malta, it was "ordinary people" who made the end of the Cold War happen: the Hungarians who declared their barbed wire obsolete and then flocked to a funeral for a man who had been dead thirty-one years, the Poles who surprised Solidarity by sweeping it into office; the east Germans who vacationed in Hungary, climbed embassy fences in Prague, humiliated Honecker at his own parade, persuaded the police not to fire in Leipzig, and ultimately opened a gate that took down a wall and reunited a country [2]. We Americans can outcompete any country, including the PRC, by showing that our system is better.

This book is a forewarning of the real possibility and immense cost of war between the US and China. The Vietnam War cost America much more than American lives lost and treasures squandered. It hurt our values, our international standing, and our domestic agendas and programs. The Cold War showed us the pitfalls of unchecked military buildup and escalation, and the matchless merit of proving our worth through the power of our examples. With chapters on Chinese Americans, IP theft, economics and trade, human rights, and Taiwan, this book illuminates how our hysteria over China is already hurting our values, our competitiveness, and ushering us on the path to war. Left unexamined or unaltered, the errors of the past will likely repeat themselves, except on a much grander and more frightful scale.

References

1. Halberstam D (1972) The Best and the Brightest. Random House, New York
2. Gaddis JL (2005) The Cold War: A New History. Penguin Press, New York
3. Stimson Center (2024) America's nuclear weapons quagmire. Available at: https://www.stimson.org/2024/americas-nuclear-weapons-quagmire/. Accessed 12 Aug 2025

CHAPTER 3

The Chinese in America

Most books on US–China relations dedicate voluminous pages to the history and present political situation of China. As the military strategist Sun Tzu—who legends say in his nearly 40 years as general, never lost a battle, campaign or war—famously uttered, "if you know the enemy and know yourself, you need not fear the result of a hundred battles. If you know yourself but not the enemy, for every victory gained you will also suffer a defeat. If you know neither the enemy nor yourself, you will succumb in every battle." Yet very seldom do any of the books explore what our own assumptions about the "Chinese," many of them harkening back centuries, have been and still are. Most Americans have never been to China and likely never will. As Chinese Americans and by extension Asian Americans are the only people who look Chinese in America, how they have been perceived and treated speaks volumes about American assumptions about the Chinese, China, and US–China relations. It is worthwhile to explore our own assumptions so that we may know ourselves better before we engage in any struggle of existential consequences.

Before I officially started as President of the Committee of 100, I was informed that my first assignment would be to tell the story of the Chinese in America. Key Committee of 100 members had recognized that the relationship between the US and China is now fundamentally altered, and that as Chinese Americans, we must not only fight for our

Z. Z. Huang, *Rethinking China*,
https://doi.org/10.1007/978-981-95-3608-5_3

rights as citizens, but to tell our story as Americans. With generous donations from members, I was given a budget of $1 million to select the best partner to articulate our story—the history of Chinese in America. I met with organizations as wide ranging as Pew Research Center, Nielsen, Eurasia Group, McKinsey & Co, and many others. We settled on the Economist Intelligence Unit, the research arm of the Economist Group, for its global and non-partisan brand as well as its keen interest in the project. As I worked closely with the team at the Economist Intelligence Unit, and the many experts that we brought on to inform our work, I discovered that there was so much I did not know about my community, and about our integral role in American history. Central to our story is not just that the Chinese were the first ethnicity specifically barred from entering the US or becoming Americans through the Chinese Exclusion Act of 1882, or that we suffered our share of pogroms and persecutions, but that despite these challenges and obstacles, Chinese Americans have contributed mightily to the making of America, from building the transatlantic railroad to helping the nation secure its leadership in space and high technology. Yet old tropes die hard, and if we are to advance our values and interests in our relations with the PRC, we must ensure that the lessons of our own history are not forgotten and that the mistakes of the past are not repeated.

Assumption #1: Yellow Peril
Assumption #2: Dual Loyalty
Assumption #3: Perpetual Foreigner

My father came to study in the US in 1980. Like many first-generation immigrants, he had to juggle multiple jobs to pay for his studies—going to school during the day and working as a motel manager at night. My mother and I joined him 7 years later. One evening shortly after our arrival, my mother decided to cook some soup and bring it to my father as a surprise. It was around ten o'clock at night, and the streets in downtown Los Angeles were deserted. Some minutes into our trip, we walked past Hilton Checkers, a historic hotel in downtown Los Angeles, and out of the hotel came a couple, hand in hand in gallant evening gowns. We walked a few paces in front, while the regal couple trailed us by two bodies' lengths. Suddenly, in a blurred sequence, I thought I heard the crackling of firecrackers, and saw a car screeching by. Then shrill screams filled the air. I turned around and caught the woman lying limp in a gushing pool of red and the man frantically yelling for help. I was no longer in China. As our frantic flight slowed into an aimless amble, as my pounding heart gave way to belabored breaths, I became more and more absorbed in one overriding inquiry. In America—the land of dreams and opportunities—what are the assumptions that guide people's actions and their intended and unintended consequences?

The Chinese are among the first non-native people of color to arrive in America, with a history of immigration stretching back over 170 years. Chinese Americans, alongside other immigrant groups, have played an important role in the building of America and the shaping of its economic, social, and institutional fabric. Chinese Americans form a diverse group, crossing every economic and social stratum. Today, they live in all 50 states, ranging from first-generation immigrants to fifth- or sixth-generation descendants, and represent great socioeconomic diversity. While the majority of Chinese Americans aged 25 and older have a bachelor's degree or above—compared with a third of Americans in the same age cohort—20% of Chinese Americans aged five and older do not speak proficient English, double the share among Americans in general. Although the community overall has an income level above the national average, roughly one in ten households earns less than $15,000 per year and 35% have incomes below the national median. Chinese Americans are active across varied professions in both the public and private sectors. This diversity is a result of the community's immigration and integration history, which has intertwined with legal and social evolutions in American society as well as geopolitical shifts.

The US made its first attempt to restrict immigration by race in the 1880s, influenced by a combination of racial tensions, labor unrest, and an increase in Chinese immigration in the previous decades. Passed in 1882, the Chinese Exclusion Act set the tone for nearly a century of legal measures designed to limit Asian immigration to the country. Many Chinese immigrants were contracted laborers who worked in West Coast industries like mining, agriculture, and railroad construction. Because they could be paid significantly less than white laborers, they were often favored when companies looked to cut costs or replace workers on strike. This practice led to widespread sentiment that Chinese laborers were stealing jobs from white laborers. Moreover, white Americans saw Chinese immigrants as unsuitable for assimilation. Anti-Chinese sentiment became more widespread after an economic downturn in the 1870s, which prompted the question of how to deal with the Chinese laborers who were supposedly stealing jobs and depressing wages. For many white Americans, the answer to the "Chinese Question" could be found in Chinese Exclusion, which intended to force Chinese laborers from their jobs, their communities, and the country, either through litigation or violence [1].

At the root of Chinese Exclusion lies the belief in the "Yellow Peril." The term Yellow Peril refers to Western fears that Asians, in particular the Chinese, would invade their lands and disrupt Western values, such as democracy, Christianity, and technological innovation. Media portrayals of Asians and Asian Americans invoked Yellow Peril imagery as a sign of villainy, malevolence, or undesirability. Popular illustrations emphasized "exotic" features, such as eye shape (often rendered as narrow slits) and skin color (often exaggeratedly yellow) [2]. According to the famed orator of the time, Horace Greeley, "the Chinese are uncivilized, unclean, and filthy beyond all conception without any of the higher domestic or social relations; lustful and sensual in their dispositions; every female is a prostitute of the basest order." This idea of an "Asian menace" was later applied to the Japanese, particularly after Japan's victory over Russia, in the Russo-Japanese War of 1904–5. According to the historian John Dower, "the vision of the menace from the East was always more racial rather than national. It derived not from concern with any one country or people in particular, but from a vague and ominous sense of the vast, faceless, nameless yellow horde: the rising tide, indeed, of color." This feeling of impending doom from the East led to the 1917 Immigration Restriction Act and the National Origins Act of 1924, two acts that prevented nearly all Asian immigrants from legally entering the US and prohibited immigrants already in the US from attaining citizenship [3].

In crafting the Committee of 100's US–China diplomatic language guide that was distributed widely within the US government, we included current examples of the century old trope. They were not hard to find. Statements such as "China threatens everything about the American way of life," "The Chinese people are fierce and untrustworthy," "First the Chinese will steal your job, then they'll hold you hostage for the widgets they made" abound [4]. One scholar who advised us on the guide pointed us to the prolific use of the word "malign," or "malignant" whenever in reference to China. As the subsequent pages illustrate, there are real and substantive concerns that the US has with the PRC government, yet it serves neither our values nor interests to fall so easily and unaware into the Yellow Peril trope. Strategic de-coupling easily veers into exclusion and discrimination when caught unaware.

Under the Chinese Exclusion Act of 1882, Chinese immigrants were prohibited from becoming citizens and hence denied the right to vote, giving them no political power to contest unfair treatment. Instead, Chinese Americans turned to the legal system to fight discriminatory immigration and citizenship laws. Their pursuit of civil rights and social justice in the 1800s established many landmark legal precedents that would significantly shape American democracy. In 1880, San Francisco passed an ordinance requiring laundries in wooden buildings to have a permit. The San Francisco Board of Supervisors had complete discretion over who would receive a permit. Of the 240 of the 310 laundries in San Francisco owned by a Chinese, none received a permit. Yick Wo was a laundry facility owned by Lee Yick, a Chinese immigrant. Yick sued for a writ of habeas corpus after he was imprisoned for refusing to pay a fine for allegedly violating the ordinance. In 1886, the Supreme Court ruled in favor of Yick Wo, ruling that it was unconstitutional to discriminate against a group of people in the passage or enforcement of legislation. The case was the first in a long series of cases to use the "equal protection" clause of the Fourteenth Amendment, and the decision opened the doors for immigrant integration into American society and established an important precedent for subsequent cases. By the 1950s, the Supreme Court had used the principle established in Yick Wo to strike down several attempts by states and municipalities in the Deep South to limit the political rights of Black Americans. To date, the Yick Wo case has been cited over 150 times in civil rights proceedings since the original decision.

Wong Kim Ark, a San Francisco born Chinese American, was barred from entering the US upon returning from China in 1894, on the grounds that he was not a US citizen under the Chinese Exclusion Act. Eventually, the Supreme Court ruled in favor of Wong, stating that children born in the US to non-citizen parents are automatically granted citizenship under the Fourteenth Amendment to the Constitution. The decision established birthright citizenship—one of the cornerstones of American identity—having an untold impact on immigrant families of all backgrounds and ethnicities, including the many generations of Americans descended from English, Scotch, Irish, German, and other European immigrants.

From 1865 to 1869, as many as 20,000 Chinese workers were employed by the Central Pacific Railroad, making up 90% of the construction workforce. Building the western half of the railroad, Chinese workers held jobs including blacksmithing, carpentry, tunneling, leveling of roadbeds, and laying tracks. Within just 10 years of its completion, the railroad was shipping $50 million worth of freight from coast to coast ($1.3 billion in today's dollars). After completing the first transcontinental railroad in 1869, Chinese workers fanned out across the country to work on at least 70 other rail lines. Today, freight railroads remain a mainstay of the US economy, moving nearly 40% of the nation's goods each year and supporting 1.5 million jobs. When the first Chinese immigrants arrived during the Gold Rush, California relied on agriculture imports to meet the food demands of a fast-growing population. Drawing from their experience in controlling waterways and developing fertile farmland in inaccessible river valleys in China, Chinese immigrants were hired to reclaim swamplands in the Sacramento-San Joaquin Delta. By 1880, they had reclaimed 88,000 acres for agricultural use, a project that increased the land value from $1–3 an acre to $20–100 an acre. The work of Chinese immigrants is also credited with facilitating the establishment of the Californian wine industry. It is estimated that viticulture in California, which today produces 90% of all wine made in the US, would have been set back 30–50 years without the contribution of Chinese vineyard workers.

Despite their vital contribution to the construction of the transcontinental railroad, Chinese workers were excluded from news reports and photographs documenting its completion, from nearly all written histories, and from twentieth century commemorations of its completion. Only in 2014 did the US Department of Labor induct Chinese railroad workers into its Hall of Fame for "their efforts, which connected the western United States to the eastern United States, laid the foundation for the extraordinary economic prosperity enjoyed by the United States in the years that followed." While Chinese workers were well represented in agricultural activities in the early decades of Chinese immigration, their participation in agriculture rapidly declined after the Chinese Exclusion Act. The decline intensified when the California Alien Land Law of 1913 prohibited "aliens ineligible for citizenship" from owning land or property. The California law, followed by similar discriminatory laws in other Western states, resulted in a virtual stoppage of Chinese American participation in agriculture. Today, as will be discussed in a subsequent chapter,

Alien Land Acts targeting the Chinese are once again proliferating across American states.

The US' investment in infrastructure after World War II—including interstate highways, airports, and port facilities, among others—set the foundation for the country's economic growth. During this period of infrastructure development, Chinese Americans—in particular civil engineers, architects, and scientists—made notable contributions. One of the most important materials in modern construction is prestressed concrete, which has made possible the construction of structures including high-rise skyscrapers and long-span bridges. Although the material was first invented in Europe, its widespread adoption in the US is attributed to the efforts of Tung-Yen (T.Y.) Lin, a visionary structural engineer best known for his pioneering work in developing prestressed concrete for practical use and his advocacy for the material's use in modern buildings. Lin led research to simplify the use of prestressed concrete and helped convene the first World Conference on Prestressed Concrete in San Francisco in 1957. Whereas 2% of the bridges built prior to the 1956 Highway Act utilized prestressed concrete as their primary superstructure elements, the number grew to nearly 50% by the beginning of the twenty-first century. In the field of bridge design, Man-Chung Tang was a world authority on cable-stayed bridges, a cost-effective design that has gained popularity since the late twentith century. Tang worked on more than 100 bridges worldwide, including the eastern segment of the San Francisco-Oakland Bay Bridge, designed to withstand the strongest seismic motion in a 1500-year period. In urban planning, Weiming Lu was instrumental in a number of urban renewal projects in Los Angeles, Minneapolis, and Dallas, among other cities. In St. Paul in the early 1970s, Lu presided over an effort to transform empty warehouses and parking lots in the historic Lowertown to a new urban village. The project yielded 2600 housing units and retained 12,000 jobs. In Dallas, Lu led an urban design effort that helped save the Texas School Book Depository, rejuvenated the West End District, created the Art District, saved Swiss Avenue, and protected the city's escarpment district and flood plain. As of 2018, 2.6% of Americans working in civil and environmental engineering are Chinese American [5].

Yet despite their contributions, Chinese and Asian Americans still suffer under the century old trope of harboring "dual loyalty." The phrase dual loyalty has its origins as an anti-Semitic canard in old Europe. The idea that a citizen of any state has a second, conflicting allegiance to another authority has often been evoked against Jewish Americans, as well as other minorities, such as John F. Kennedy when he ran as an Irish Catholic for the American Presidency. Over the past century, the dual loyalty trope has been used repeatedly against the Asian American community. Allegations of dual loyalty separate Asian Americans from other ethnic minorities. African Americans face systemic, often violent racism, yet that experience is not contingent on the US' relationship with African countries. Hispanic Americans, too, are victims of discrimination, but that does not depend on who is serving as president of Mexico, Honduras, or Argentina. Yet for Asian Americans, the United States' strained relations with major Asian powers, such as the PRC, directly lead to claims of dual loyalty being levied against them [6].

On February 19, 1942, following the attack by Imperial Japan on Pearl Harbor and the United States' entry to WWII, President Franklin D. Roosevelt signed Executive Order 9066, which led to the forced removal and incarceration of over 120,000 individuals of Japanese ancestry [7]. From the extreme heat of the Gila River in Arizona, to the biting winters of Heart Mountain in Wyoming, Japanese Americans were forced into hastily built barracks, with no insulation or privacy, and surrounded by barbed wire. They shared bathrooms and mess halls, and families of up to eight were squeezed into 20-by-25-foot rooms. Armed soldiers in guard towers ensured nobody tried to flee. Approximately two-thirds of the detainees were American citizens. All the while, during World War II, an estimated 33,000 Japanese Americans served in the US military.

Senator Andy Kim represents New Jersey. Prior to his congressional win, he worked as a career public servant under both Democrats and Republicans, having served at USAID, the Pentagon, the State Department, the White House National Security Council, and in Afghanistan as an advisor to Generals Petraeus and Allen [8]. He has spoken frequently and publicly about how he was denied assignments on Korea while at the State Department because he is Korean American, and deemed a national security risk. In our many conversations, he bemoaned the fact that the dual loyalty trope endures, and handicaps America's global interests when Americans with the requisite linguistic, cultural, and relational understandings are passed over because they are presumed to harbor dual loyalties. It is hard for the Chinese American community to not feel targeted when the Justice Department sets up an initiative called the China initiative targeting one specific country, and nearly 90% of the defendants charged under the initiative are of Chinese heritage [9].

In speaking with people from all walks of life in the Chinese American community, I came away with the appreciation that for those who made a conscious decision to become American, their faith in and commitment to America is often greater because they had to make that choice deliberately, oftentimes with great sacrifice and peril. The more welcoming and trusting the US has been to the Chinese, as with other immigrant groups, the more it has benefited from their presence.

During the COVID-19 pandemic I took frequent walks in the Marina district in San Francisco. One day while I was strolling in Crissy Fields, with the Golden Gate Bridge glistening through the mist, I was jolted to reality when two elderly white women, seated on a park bench, yelled, "Go back to your country!" For a minute I paused, looked at them, and wanted to scream out, "this is my country." The perpetual foreigner stereotype posits that members of ethnic minorities will always be seen as the "other" in the white dominant society of the US. "Where are you from?" This benign question is commonly asked during social interactions, and the answer often leads to interesting conversations with strangers or acquaintances. But what if an answer like "Lincoln, Nebraska," "Baltimore, Maryland," or "San Francisco, California" does not suffice for the questioner? Indeed, ethnic minorities, especially Asian Americans, are often asked follow-up questions like, "No, where are you *really* from?" or "I meant, where are you *originally* from [10]?" A 2023 survey conducted by the Pew Research Center found that about eight-in-ten Asian Americans (78%) have experienced at least one of the following incidents in their day-to-day interactions: 68% of Asian adults say people have mispronounced their name, 39% say people have acted as if they didn't speak English, 32% say people have told them to go back to their "home country," 22% say people have criticized them for speaking a language other than English in public [11].

Arts and culture are vital to the creation of a common national identity. A robust and vibrant culture, driven by diverse and creative minds, increases a society's wellbeing and opens up new avenues for innovation and growth. As a nation built by immigrants, one of the greatest assets of America is the breadth of artistic experiences arising from its diverse population. Alongside Americans of every race and background, Chinese Americans have utilized their talents to help enrich American culture and shape its social fabric. For centuries, Chinese American creatives have had to counter the assumption that race and ethnicity indelibly mark artistic production, and thus artists of Asian descent have to produce art that is somehow inherently "Asian" in terms of themes or aesthetic.

World War II, an armed conflict colored by ideologies, marked a seismic shift in the value of arts and culture as a social and political tool. American artists supported the war effort in numerous and important ways. Artists not only helped to create extensive pictorial records of the war, they also aided local and national campaigns to boost troop morale, sell war bonds, and encourage national unity. Depictions of the war's battlefields and life at home crystallized American culture and reinforced a vision of a patriotic and democratic people. Throughout the war, Chinese American artists, actors, and filmmakers helped to construct images of a national self. Several well-known Chinese American artists found their work in high demand. One example is Dong Kingman, often described as America's most popular watercolorist in the mid-twentieth century. Kingman was drafted into the US army in 1944, but Eleanor Roosevelt, a fan of Kingman's work, arranged for his transfer to the Art Department of the OSS, a precursor to the CIA, where he drew maps and charts. Kingman was an especially talented painter of quotidian American life. His watercolor paintings of American cityscapes and countryside, with their bold colors and unusual use of line that integrated Chinese and Western brush and paint techniques, contributed to the visualization of an American national identity. Another Chinese American artist influential during the war was James Wong Howe, one of the world's leading cinematographers in the prewar period. During World War II, Howe made documentary style films such as Air Force (1943) and Objective Burma! (1945) that helped the American public imagine the Pacific battlefield. His work during these years confirmed his reputation as a pioneer of realism in American cinema.

Chinese Americans have been active participants in American arts and culture since their arrival in the early 1800s, although the artistic focus has shifted and expanded over time. In the earlier years, due to the social, legal, and professional discrimination they faced, Chinese American artists often focused on their own communities, depicting Chinese immigrants and their lives. Early creative pursuits, such as the many Chinese theatres and pan-Asian art exhibits in San Francisco, though inward facing, were crucial in shaping the US as a melting pot of artistic styles and influences. As American cultural consciousness turned towards diversity in the twentieth century, Chinese American creatives began to bring broader themes into their work. In literature, Amy Tan's novels, including *The*

Joy Luck Club, employed stories of Chinese Americans to explore themes familiar to all Americans such as faith, family, loss, motherhood, and the stark cultural differences often found between generations of families descended from immigrants.

In more recent decades, Chinese American writers have helped bridge the gap between foreign language books and American readers. In 2014, Chinese American novelist Ken Liu published a translation of a Chinese science fiction novel, *The Three-Body Problem*, which was hailed as a groundbreaking work by readers ranging from President Obama to George RR Martin. In 2015 *The Three-Body* Problem became the first translated novel to win the Hugo Award, the genre's most prestigious honor. In other areas, architect I.M. Pei integrated Western modernist architecture with myriad cultural traditions. In the 1960s, Pei designed the multi-airline terminal at John F Kennedy International Airport in New York City, known as the "Sundrome." Pei's innovative East Building (1978) of the National Gallery of Art, Washington D.C., an elegant triangular composition, remains a staple of the capital's public arts infrastructure [5]. In filmmaking, Ang Lee, known for movies including *Life of Pi*, *Brokeback Mountain* and *Crouching Tiger, Hidden Dragon*, wove together themes of multiculturalism and migration, achieving critical acclaim in the process. Meanwhile, younger generations of Chinese American artists have emerged in a variety of media. Ali Wong, a comedian, writer, and actress, is best known for her groundbreaking Netflix standup specials *Baby Cobra* and *Hard Knock Wife*. Awkwafina, an actress and rapper, continues to push the creative envelope. Alongside a broadening contribution to American performing arts and creative media, Chinese Americans are increasingly assuming roles in journalism, reporting on subjects ranging from financial and business news to societal developments and trends. The lessons of history seem incontrovertible: when America falls under the sway of century old tropes—the Yellow Peril, Dual Loyalty, and Perpetual Foreigner—American values and interests suffer. When America rises above them, all Americans benefit.

Better assumptions can be:

> Assumption #1: Diversity is our Core Value and the Source of our Competitiveness
>
> Assumption #2: Chinese in America are a National Security Asset, not Liability

Assumption #3: Chinese Immigrants and Ideas are Integral to the Success of America

Sometime ago I had lunch with a dear friend, David Lei, a noted community leader and amateur historian from San Francisco. Between bites of dim sum, David asked, "we are having food in Burlingame, California, do you know anything about the city's namesake, Anson Burlingame?" Gulping down my pork dumplings, I replied, "No, pray do tell." Born in 1820, Anson Burlingame was a Republican lawyer and Congressman from Massachusetts. In 1861, he was appointed by President Abraham Lincoln to be the first US Minister Plenipotentiary to China, working under Secretary of State William Seward to establish the US as a power in the Asia Pacific. The US wanted to gain access to profitable trading opportunities in China and foster the spread of Christianity and other Western ideas. The Qing court at the time was encouraged to send reciprocal diplomatic missions abroad. Burlingame's stay in China was so successful, and the trust he built was so enduring, that the Chinese asked that Burlingame represent China as envoy extraordinary on a world tour that included Washington, London, Paris, and Berlin. Burlingame received a special dispensation from the US government to assist the Chinese in their treaty negotiations with Secretary of State Seward.

The Burlingame-Seward Treaty was signed in 1868. The first articles of the treaty protected commerce conducted in Chinese ports and cities and established the right of China to appoint consuls to American port cities. The more groundbreaking articles included measures that promised the Chinese the right to free immigration and travel within the US and allowed for the protection of Chinese citizens in the US in accordance with the most-favored-nation principle. Another article gave citizens of the two nations reciprocal access to education and schooling when living in the other country. All of these articles served to reinforce the principle of equality between the two nations. The migration of Chinese to America began in earnest because of the Burlingame-Seward Treaty [12].

Today, science and technology are the cornerstones of the US economy and at the heart of the competition between the US and PRC. The past century has seen remarkable increases in Chinese Americans' contributions to American science and technology, thanks to the repeal of discriminatory laws and anti-immigration policies beginning in the 1940s. A growing number of Chinese came to study in the US in the postwar period—first from Taiwan and Hong Kong and later from mainland

China—eventually settling and becoming US citizens [13]. As of 2018, 15% of working Chinese Americans are employed in the life, physical, and social sciences, computing and mathematics, and architecture and engineering—nearly three times as high as Americans in general. Between 1998 and 2018, more than 288,000 Chinese American students obtained bachelor's degrees or above in science, technology, engineering, and mathematics. The Committee of 100 membership is full of such extraordinary Americans. One person I dearly wish to have met, but who passed away in 1997, is Chien-Shiung Wu, a co-founder of the Committee. When Chien-Shiung was born in China 100 years ago, most girls did not attend school; no one considered them as smart as boys. But her parents felt differently. Giving her a name meaning "courageous hero," they encouraged her love of learning and science. She enrolled at the University of California Berkeley in 1936 for her PhD in Physics and over her long career, battled sexism and racism to become what *Newsweek* magazine called the "Queen of Physics." Along the way, she earned the admiration of famous scientists like Enrico Fermi and Robert Oppenheimer and became the sole Chinese American woman physicist who worked on the Manhattan Project that produced the atomic bomb, first woman hired as an instructor by Princeton University, first woman elected President of the American Physical Society, first scientist to have an asteroid named after her when she was still alive, first elected Chinese American member of the National Academy of Science in the 1950s, and many other honors [14]. In February 2021, Chien-Shiung was honored on a US Postal Service Commemorative Forever Stamp [15]. Elsewhere, during the 1960s, Wen Tsing Chow made groundbreaking advancements in the fields of computer-guided navigation and systems engineering, playing a key role in verifying the guidance equations and software implementation for NASA's Gemini manned spaceflight program. Chow's pioneering use of photochemical circuitry enabled the miniaturization of computer components in guidance systems, which made possible digital computers in missiles and spacecraft. His work also paved the way for further microminiaturization, as is used in most technology products today.

Very few Americans today can imagine life without mobile devices, computers, or the internet. The digital world we live in has been driven by breakthroughs in semiconductor and computing in the 1960s, the invention and evolution of the internet and personal computers in the 1970s–2000s, and the recent rise and proliferation of smart devices, social media, and artificial intelligence. One in ten of the National Academy of Engineering's elected members in the field of electronics, communication, and information is Chinese American. Two in 25 (7.8%) electrical and electronics engineers and materials engineers working in the manufacturing of computer, communications, and electronic components and parts are Chinese American. The digital revolution would have been impossible without breakthroughs in semiconductor technology. In 1963, while working at Fairchild Semiconductor Corporation, Chih-Tang Sah invented the complementary metal–oxide–semiconductor (CMOS) device fabrication process. Today, CMOS technology is used to manufacture more than 90% of integrated circuits, which make up mobile phones, computers, televisions, and a wide array of consumer electronics integral to American life. Other notable contributors include Chenming Hu, whose work on metal oxide semiconductor (MOS) reliability and device modeling has had an enormous impact on the continued scaling of electronic devices, enabling smaller yet more functional and higher performance integrated circuits; Robert S Chau, who played a key role at Intel in advancing revolutionary changes in transistor technology that enabled smaller, faster, and more energy efficient microprocessors; and Burn Jeng Lin, a leading figure in semiconductor manufacturing renowned for his contributions to lithographic manufacturing.

The so-called Fourth Industrial Revolution is a confluence of technological breakthroughs including artificial intelligence, robotics, the Internet of Things, biotechnology, 3-D printing, and autonomous vehicles, among others. Together, these technologies hold the potential of disrupting every industry and transforming entire systems of production, management, and governance. Whether the US can stay at the forefront of these technologies will determine its global stature in the coming decades. Chinese Americans have been at the heart of advancing these technologies. Working in AI and machine learning, Fei-Fei Li, a computer scientist and professor at Stanford University, was elected to the National Academy of Engineering in 2020 for her contributions to "building large knowledge bases for machine learning and visual understanding." Andrew Ng founded and directed the Google Brain Deep Learning Project in the early 2010s. In bioengineering, Yulun Wang invented the first FDA approved surgical robot, a voice controlled robotic arm that can hold and move a laparoscope (a tool used in keyhole surgery) for a surgeon. Wang also developed the ZEUS robotic surgical system, which performed the world's first trans-Atlantic surgery.

Through the Committee of 100's work documenting the story of the Chinese in America, it became crystal clear to me that for America to maintain our global leadership, diversity is not only good in words but the true source of our competitiveness. For too long Americans have been fed the assumption that left unchecked, a foreign people or thought can bring about the utter destruction of the American civilization. The Yellow Peril trope rests on the assumption that Asians, in particular, the Chinese, are an existential threat to Western civilization because of their differing cultural, political, or social practices. In 1989, political scientist Francis Fukuyama argued that history should be viewed as an evolutionary process, and that the end of history means that liberal democracy is the final form of government for all nations. Fast forward three plus decades, the world seems more diverse in political thought and social structures. For America, diversity is our core value and the source of our competitiveness. It is critical to examine carefully any assumption—toward the Chinese or any other ethnicity—that reflexively equates otherness with peril to our way of life.

National security is at the heart of a nation's interests. It serves as the foundation for prosperity and well-being. Alongside Americans of every race and ethnicity, Chinese Americans have demonstrated their loyalty to the nation by fighting for its security and freedom in every crucial moment in history—from the Civil War to World War II to the War on Terror—and have contributed across the national security apparatus. As of 2018, approximately 75,000 living Chinese Americans (or one in 40 Chinese Americans aged 17 years or older) have previously served in the US military or are currently on active duty or in training in the Reserves and National Guard. More than 15,000 Chinese Americans serve in the intelligence community as of 2018. In particular, one in 20 computer and information research scientists and one in 40 interpreters and translators are Chinese American [16].

One out of every five Chinese American men (more than 20,000 individuals) served in the US Armed Forces during World War II. Many were initially denied the opportunity to serve on the basis of their ethnicity, until General Henry Arnold, commander of the US Army during World War II, opened up enlistment to Chinese American volunteers. In the Air Force, Sergeant Thomas Fong received the Air Medal for outstanding service in the bomber corps over Europe and Lieutenant Colonel Frank Fong received the same for commanding the Fifth Emergency Rescue Squadron that rescued US and Allied aircrews downed in the North

Sea. In the Navy, Rear Admiral Gordon Chung-Hoon, the first Chinese American to command a Navy warship, commanded the USS Sigsbee (a destroyer) in the Pacific campaign. In 1945, the destroyer assisted in the destruction of 20 enemy planes while screening a carrier strike force off the Japanese island of Kyushu. Admiral Chung-Hoon was awarded the Navy Cross and Silver Star for his heroism. In the army, Francis B Wai received the Medal of Honor—the nation's highest military decoration for bravery. Serving in the Philippines in 1944, Captain Wai landed on the island of Leyte and immediately assumed command of a disorganized group of American soldiers. Under heavy machine gun and rifle fire, he moved inland without cover. His soldiers, inspired by his courage, rose from their positions and followed him. During the advance, Captain Wai was killed in the line of duty while leading an assault upon the last remaining enemy stronghold in the area. Chinese American women also made important contributions. Hazel (Ying) Lee and Maggie Gee joined the Women Air Force Service Pilots (WASP) to work with the Air Force to ferry planes from factories to air bases and test planes for mechanical problems. Chinese American women also provided translation and interpretation services within the Women's Army Corp and served in the Army Nursing Corps.

Chinese Americans fought for the US in every major military conflict in the twentieth century, from the Korean War to the War in Vietnam to the Gulf War. Major Kurt Chew-Een Lee, the first Chinese American officer in the Marine Corps, led Marines into battle in the Korean War and was cited for bravery for helping to preserve a crucial evacuation route for 8000 American troops. In 1950, Major Lee conducted a solo reconnaissance mission in heavy snow, moving ahead of his unit to fire rounds and throw grenades to expose the location of enemy soldiers. He was wounded, but his tactics worked, allowing his unit to reposition and drive back enemy troops. Major Lee was awarded the Navy Cross, the second highest honor in the Marine Corps, for "extraordinary heroism." As of 2018, one in 40 first-line supervisors of mechanics, installers, and repairers in the US Army is Chinese American; one in 50 healthcare practitioners and technical personnel serving in the US military is Chinese American. One example of such support is Colonel Geoffrey Ling, who specializes in traumatic brain injury and prostheses, two areas of medical practice that provide veterans and active duty servicemembers with life changing care. For years, Colonel Ling was the Army's only neuro-intensive specialist and was considered to be its premier authority on Traumatic Brain Injury

(TBI). TBI has been called the "signature injury" of Afghanistan and Iraq, and the Defense and Veterans Brain Injury Center has reported nearly 350,000 diagnoses of TBI in the US military since 2000. In addition to his work with TBIs, Colonel Ling is also known for advances in the development of prosthetic limbs. He launched the Revolutionizing Prosthetics Program in 2006, leading a research team to develop high tech prosthetic limb replacements, including an advanced electromechanical prosthetic upper limb. The technology, which received approval from the US Food and Drug Administration (FDA) in 2014, helps those who have lost limbs—civilians as well as veterans—to regain independence and enjoy improved quality of life.

Although underrepresented at the highest echelons, several Chinese Americans have managed to break the glass ceiling and assume senior leadership roles in the US military. In 1980, Rear Admiral Ming Chang became the first naturalized Chinese American naval officer to reach flag rank; during his 34 years of military service, he received the Legion of Merit (Combat V) and Bronze Star (Combat V) medals. In 1984, former Committee of 100 Chair John L. Fugh became the first Chinese American to reach the rank of Major General. He served in the Army Corps' top post, the Judge Advocate General (TJAG), from 1991 to 1993. During his career, Major General Fugh enacted a number of important and lasting reforms. He introduced the Army's first environmental law division and established its procurement fraud division. During the Gulf War, Major General Fugh established a human rights training program and published the War Crimes Report—the first American effort since World War II to systematically document enemy war crimes.

Over the past decades, the US government has established various advisory groups to provide independent scientific and technical advice on matters critical to national security. These groups typically consist of experts from industry, national laboratories, academia, and retired military officer corp. Heidi Shyu, a former Raytheon executive, provided guidance to the US Air Force first as a member of the US Air Force Scientific Advisory Board from 2000 to 2010, and later, in her role as the Assistant Secretary of the Army for Acquisition, Logistics, and Technology. Elsewhere, the Central Intelligence Agency (CIA) created a venture capital arm called In-Q-Tel in 1999 to help identify and invest in startups that serve national security interests. Gilman Louie, a fourth-generation Chinese American who grew up in a military family in San Francisco, founded In-Q-Tel, and served as its first CEO until 2006.

Under his leadership, In-Q-Tel invested in over 80 companies that have had a significant impact on national security. In 2003, the firm invested in Keyhole, a pioneer of interactive 3D earth visualization that became Google Earth the following year. Within 2 weeks of acquiring the technology, the Pentagon and the National Imagery and Mapping Agency began using it to support troops in Iraq.

Chinese in America are a national security asset, not a liability. In May 2022, the Office of the Director of National Intelligence published a "Best Practices to Protect Privacy, Civil Liberties, and Civil Rights of Americans of Chinese Descent in the Conduct of U.S. Intelligence Activities." The Report clearly states that "conducting intelligence activities or subjecting individuals to greater scrutiny during the security background process based upon race or ethnicity does not reflect the Intelligence Community's commitment to objective intelligence collection. Moreover, as discussed in this report, it is the Intelligence Community's assessment that the PRC's foreign intelligence services prioritize other factors over race or ethnicity when those services evaluate the potential recruitment of human assets [17]." Yet the dual loyalty trope persists. Perhaps one of the most notorious examples is a case involving Dr. Wen Ho Lee, a physicist at Los Alamos National Laboratory in New Mexico. In 1999, Lee was charged with sending US nuclear secrets to the PRC and held in solitary confinement with constant shackling for 9 months. Eventually, the case against Lee unraveled, and in September 2000 he was acquitted of 58 of the 59 charges against him and later awarded $1.6 million in damages. The Judge in the case, James A. Parker of the Federal District Court in Albuquerque, New Mexico, wrote to Lee that "although, as I indicated, I have no authority to speak on behalf of the executive branch, the President, the Vice President, the Attorney General, or the Secretary of the Department of Energy, as a member of the third branch of the United States Government, the judiciary, the United States Courts, I sincerely apologize to you, Dr. Lee, for the unfair manner you were held in custody by the executive branch [18]." As noted by the scientific journal Nature in February 2024, 2 years after the end of the China Initiative, Chinese American academics continue to describe being treated like spies, resulting in a loss of talent and a chilling atmosphere that is stifling American science [19]. I believe history informs us that we can compete with the PRC government, at the same time trust and rely on Chinese Americans, and continue to welcome Chinese immigrants to study and invest in America. It is in accordance with our values and firmly in our national interest to clearly delineate among Chinese Americans, the Chinese people, and the PRC government. For while we may take strong issues with the actions of the PRC government, the more welcoming and trusting we have been of the Chinese, the more America has benefited, including in national security.

Public health is essential to American well-being and national competitiveness. As of 2018, more than 240,000—or one in ten—Chinese Americans in the workforce are employed in healthcare and health support occupations. The majority are healthcare practitioners, with outsized representation as optometrists, pharmacists, dentists, surgeons, and physicians. Roughly one in 20 healthcare practitioners across these occupations is Chinese American. In addition, Chinese Americans represent a major force in driving scientific research and pharmaceutical development. As of 2018, there were more than 16,000 Chinese American biological scientists, medical scientists, and other life scientists—accounting for 7% of the workforce in these occupations.

But this wasn't always so. The Chinese Exclusion Act prevented Chinese Americans from acquiring medical licenses. Dr. Joseph Chak Thoms was the first Western trained Chinese physician to practice in the US. When Thoms attempted to open a medical clinic in Brooklyn in the 1890s, his immigration status prevented him from doing so. Born in China, Thoms was ineligible for American citizenship, a requirement then for obtaining professional licenses in New York and many other states. In the end, he was only permitted to treat Chinese patients. The Chinese Exclusion Act greatly limited Chinese American participation in the healthcare professions until its repeal in 1943. One of the great medical breakthroughs in the twentieth century was in the field of reproductive science. In 1978 scientists successfully created the first "test-tube baby" through In Vitro Fertilization (IVF), a breakthrough that would not have been possible without the pioneering work of Dr. Min Chue Chang, a Chinese American biologist. In 1959, Chang became the first to successfully produce healthy rabbits through IVF, a process that he would refine towards eventual human trials. Globally, more than 8 million babies have been born via IVF since 1978, while in the US roughly 1–2% of new births every year are via IVF.

The US reported its first HIV case in 1981. By 1995, HIV/AIDS was the leading cause of death among Americans aged 25–44. In the fight against the HIV/AIDS epidemic, several Chinese American researchers made remarkable contributions. In the mid-1990s, Dr. David Ho developed an HIV treatment known as combination antiretroviral therapy, which combined a cocktail of drugs that work together to help treat HIV. This treatment proved to be a turning point: Ho's therapy transformed AIDS from a fatal disease into a treatable, non-life-threatening condition. Since its implementation in 1996, combination antiretroviral therapy has significantly reduced HIV/AIDS mortality. To date, more than 25 million people worldwide have benefited from the treatment. Another Chinese American molecular biologist, Dr. Flossie Wong-Staal, played a significant role in identifying the workings of HIV and was the first to clone the virus. Outside of healthcare institutions, Chinese Americans have contributed to the fight against COVID-19 in many other ways, including the development of essential personal protective equipment (PPE). The N95 respirator, one of the most protective masks available, was invented by Peter Tsai, a Chinese American material scientist, in 1995.

According to 2018 figures, Chinese Americans account for 15% of biological, medical, and life scientists working in the pharmaceutical and medicine manufacturing industry, as well as 7% of those working in universities and scientific R&D facilities. Chinese Americans also accounted for 7% of research doctorates granted in bioengineering and biomedical engineering. One of the pioneers of bioengineering was Dr. Yuan-Cheng "Bert" Fung, widely regarded as a founding figure of bioengineering and dubbed "the father of modern biomechanics." In recognition of his exceptional contributions to the field of bioengineering, Fung was awarded the National Medal of Science in 2000. Following in Fung's footsteps, two other Chinese American scientists, Dr. Shu Chien and Dr. Van C Mow, greatly advanced the field. They both served as founding fellows of the American Institute of Medical and Biological Engineering. Chien helped to found the Department of Bioengineering at University of California, San Diego in 1994, and Mow served as the founding chair of the Department of Biomedical Engineering at Columbia University from 2000 to 2011 [20].

Growing up in Los Angeles, I spent hours each day on the dilapidated basketball court right in front of the local library. The court had a rusted hoop, no net, and cracked concrete that heated up in the summers. But that court was where I learned how to box out, hustle on defense, and take the winning shot. It was more than a place for a game. It was there I first felt what America truly meant—its values not just spoken, but lived and felt. On the court, nobody cared about my skin color, my accent, or my birthplace. What mattered was whether you showed up, played fair, looked out for your teammates, and earned your place. That's what captivated me about America—each of us makes our own court here. For some, it is a classroom, a business; for others, an art studio, or a garrison. Whatever it is, it shapes how we come to believe in this country, and truly love this country.

From my journey tracing the history of the Chinese in America, I came away convinced that America's secret to success lies in its ability to integrate the world's best talents and ideas, and then making them uniquely our own. We have taken ideas once foreign and made them American, just as we have taken people, once foreign, and made them American. To think of a people or idea as "perpetually foreign" only limits our own potential and growth. Americans today are as open to the benefits of ancient Chinese techniques such as Taichi and acupuncture as they are with advanced gene therapy. Since 1979, China has been among the world's fastest growing economies, with real annual GDP growth averaging 9.5% through 2018, a pace described by the World Bank as "the fastest sustained expansion by a major economy in history." Such growth has enabled China, on average, to double its GDP every 8 years and helped raise an estimated 800 million people out of poverty [21]. Chinese immigrants ***and*** ideas are integral to the success of America. It is in our national interest to closely examine the lessons afforded by China's myriad social and economic experiments and undertakings, to learn its best practices and avoid its pitfalls, in our competition with China or any other nation.

References

1. Library of Congress (2022) The Chinese Exclusion Act, Part 1: The history. Available at: https://blogs.loc.gov/law/2022/05/the-chinese-exclusion-act-part-1-the-history/. Accessed 12 Aug 2025
2. Bowling Green State University (n.d.) Asian immigration: The "Yellow Peril." Available at: https://digitalgallery.bgsu.edu/student/exhibits/show/race-in-us/asian-americans/asian-immigration-and-the–yel. Accessed 12 Aug 2025
3. Dartmouth College (n.d.) The malleable yet undying nature of the Yellow Peril. Available at: https://www.dartmouth.edu/~hist32/History/S22%20-The%20Malleable%20Yet%20Undying%20Nature%20of%20the%20Yellow%20Peril.htm (page no longer available). Accessed 12 Aug 2025

4. Committee of 100 (2023) Diplomatic Language Guide Memo. Available at: https://www.committee100.org/committee-of-100-diplomatic-language-guide-memo/. Accessed 12 Aug 2025
5. Committee of 100 (n.d.) Thematic report on Chinese American contributions: Infrastructure. Available at: https://www.committee100.org/our-work/from-foundations-to-frontiers/. Accessed 12 Aug 2025
6. World Politics Review (2021) Amid China–US tensions, dual loyalty rears its ugly head. Available at: https://www.worldpoliticsreview.com/amid-china-us-tensions-dual-loyalty-rears-its-ugly-head/. Accessed 12 Aug 2025
7. U.S. National Archives (2022) Executive Order 9066. Available at: https://www.archives.gov/milestone-documents/executive-order-9066. Accessed 12 Aug 2025
8. U.S. House of Representatives (n.d.) About Representative Andy Kim. Available at: https://www.kim.senate.gov/about/. Accessed 12 Aug 2025
9. MIT Technology Review (2021) The US crackdown on Chinese economic espionage is a mess. We have the data to show it. Available at: https://www.technologyreview.com/2021/12/02/1040656/china-initative-us-justice-department/. Accessed 12 Aug 2025
10. National Center for Biotechnology Information (2011) Perpetual foreigner in one's own land: Potential implications for identity and psychological adjustment. Available at: https://www.ncbi.nlm.nih.gov/pmc/articles/PMC3092701/. Accessed 12 Aug 2025
11. Pew Research Center (2023) Asian Americans and the 'forever foreigner' stereotype. Available at: https://www.pewresearch.org/race-ethnicity/2023/11/30/asian-americans-and-the-forever-foreigner-stereotype/. Accessed 12 Aug 2025
12. U.S. Department of State (n.d.) The Burlingame–Seward Treaty, 1868. Available at: https://history.state.gov/milestones/1866-1898/burlingame-seward-treaty/. Accessed 12 Aug 2025
13. Committee of 100 (n.d.) Thematic report on Chinese American contributions: Science and technology. Available at: https://www.committee100.org/our-work/from-foundations-to-frontiers/. Accessed 12 Aug 2025
14. Science Museum of Minnesota (n.d.) Queen of physics. Available at: https://store.smm.org/products/queen-of-physics. Accessed 12 Aug 2025
15. United States Postal Service (2021) Nuclear physicist Chien-Shiung Wu to be honored on Forever Stamp. Available at: https://about.usps.com/newsroom/national-releases/2021/0201ma-nuclear-physicist-chien-shiung-wu-to-be-honored-on-forever-stamp.htm. Accessed 12 Aug 2025
16. Committee of 100 (n.d.) Thematic report on Chinese American contributions: Military and national security. Available at: https://www.committee100.org/our-work/from-foundations-to-frontiers/. Accessed 12 Aug 2025

17. Office of the Director of National Intelligence (2022) Best practices to protect privacy, civil liberties, and civil rights of Americans of Chinese descent in conduct of US intelligence activities. Available at: https://www.dni.gov/files/CLPT/documents/ODNI_Report_on_Best_Practices_to_Protect_Privacy_Civil_Liberties_and_Civil_Rights_of_Americans_of_Chinese_Descent_in_ConductOof_US_Intelligence_Activities_May_2022.pdf. Accessed 12 Aug 2025
18. The New York Times (2000) Statement by judge in Los Alamos case, with apology for abuse of power. Available at: https://www.nytimes.com/2000/09/14/us/statement-by-judge-in-los-alamos-case-with-apology-for-abuse-of-power.html. Accessed 12 Aug 2025
19. Gewin V (2024) Why the US border remains 'a place of terror' for scientists of Chinese descent. Nature. Available at: https://www.nature.com/articles/d41586-024-00546-2. Accessed 12 Aug 2025
20. Committee of 100 (n.d.) Thematic report on Chinese American contributions: Public health. Available at: https://www.committee100.org/our-work/from-foundations-to-frontiers/. Accessed 12 Aug 2025
21. Congressional Research Service (2019) China's Economic Rise: History, Trends, Challenges, and Implications for the United States. Available at: https://www.everycrsreport.com/reports/RL33534.html. Accessed 12 Aug 2025

CHAPTER 4

IP Theft: The $600 Billion Myth

Assumption 1: The PRC steals $600 Billion of IP annually from the US
Assumption 2: IP theft from the PRC is state sponsored
Assumption 3: IP theft from the PRC is a whole of society attack

Intellectual property (IP) theft is at the heart of the ongoing economic and trade disputes between the US and PRC. In a series of tweets in 2019, President Trump explained his rationale for the more than $300 billion tariffs levied on Chinese goods: "For many years China (and many other countries) has been taking advantage of the United States on Trade, Intellectual Property Theft, and much more. Our country has been losing hundreds of billions of dollars a year to China, with no end in sight... As President, I can no longer allow this to happen." In 2018, The US Trade Representative's Office released the "Findings of the Investigation into China's Acts, Policies, and Practices Related to Technology Transfer, Intellectual Property, and Innovation Under Section 301 of the Trade Act of 1974," and estimated that Chinese theft of American IP stands at $225–$600 billion annually [1]. President Biden has elected to continue the trade tariffs, in addition to export restrictions including semiconductors and microelectronics, quantum information technologies, artificial intelligence, and outbound investment controls [2].

Z. Z. Huang, *Rethinking China*,
https://doi.org/10.1007/978-981-95-3608-5_4

IP theft is a real and pressing concern. An American company may toil for years or decades on perfecting a technology, and through IP theft a competitor may not only shorten the technology gap, but directly threaten the health and viability of said company. There are well-documented cases of Americans, including naturalized citizens from China, who have been convicted in a US court of law on charges of economic espionage on behalf of the PRC. Dongfan "Greg" Chung, a former Rockwell and Boeing engineer, was convicted in 2009 of economic espionage on behalf of the PRC. During the trial, prosecution demonstrated that communications between the Chinese aviation industry and Chung may have gone back as far as 1979 [3]. In 2023, the New York Times published an article titled "The Daring Ruse that Exposed China's Campaign to Steal American Secrets," in which it described in detail the methods of a Chinese intelligence officer at the Ministry of State Security based in Jiangsu Province, China, to elicit proprietary technology from a Chinese American engineer working at GE Aviation in Cincinnati, Ohio [4]. Through an FBI sting operation, the Chinese intelligence officer, Yanjun Xu, was apprehended in a third country, brought to trial in the US, and convicted of economic espionage and trade secret theft in 2022 [5]. Through these and other cases, the FBI believes that the PRC government is coordinating a state sponsored effort to steal IP from American companies, and the bureau has focused on Chinese Americans as the primary source of suspicion.

In 2020, I attended a business forum chaired by US Ambassador to China Terry Branstad. Multiple American business owners stood up and talked about how their IP was stolen by Chinese competitors. One small business owner spoke about having to file for bankruptcy because a Chinese competitor had stolen his IP and was now selling similar products at significantly lower cost. I know this from personal experience. The financial services data company that I had started in China had faced similar problems. We had found out that a former employee had pilfered our proprietary IP and then moved to a competitor with the information. It took many gut-wrenching months during which we had to assess and stem our losses, contemplate and initiate legal actions, and rebuild our systems and technologies. I understand personally the immense cost and suffering resulting from IP theft.

US administration officials and media regularly cite the $600 billion number to decry the incredible steal perpetuated by the PRC. In a 2023 opinion piece in the Wall Street Journals titled "My Plan to Confront the Chinese Threat," former UN ambassador and Republican presidential candidate Nikki Haley referenced the $600 billion number as direct evidence of the PRC not playing by the rules, hurting American companies, and robbing American workers of jobs critical to America's future [6]. The $600 billion number, with the resultant political and economic implications, has become accepted truth across Republican and Democratic circles.

My curiosity on the matter was piqued in 2021, when I first saw the results of our research, conducted with the Committee of 100 and legal scholar Andrew Kim, that examined all cases prosecuted under the Economic Espionage Act (EEA), dating back to 1996. The EEA is a US federal law enacted in 1996 that criminalizes the theft or misappropriation of trade secrets, including "all forms and types of financial, business, scientific, technical, economic, or engineering information" that derives independent economic value from not being publicly known. The law addresses economic espionage for the benefit of foreign entities, as well as commercial theft of trade secrets regardless of the beneficiary. Titled "Racial Disparities in Economic Espionage Act Prosecutions: A Window into the New Red Scare," the research unambiguously showed that the percentage of Chinese and Asian defendants charged skyrocketed over the past decade. Prior to 2009, two-thirds of the defendants charged under the EEA were people with Western names, and only 16% were people with Chinese names. However, since 2009, the majority of people charged with EEA offenses have been people of Chinese descent. While news stories focused on espionage for China, 42% of defendants charged under the EEA were alleged to have stolen trade secrets for the benefit of an American business or person. Only 46% of alleged theft were for the benefit of China, while the remaining 12% of alleged theft were for the benefit of other countries, including Australia and Canada. Media coverage has insinuated faculty and students at American universities of acting as agents of economic espionage, yet actual charges against these defendants rarely included accusations of espionage. Only 3% of trade secret thefts alleged under the EEA occurred in research institutions. Finally, the Department of Justice issued press releases announcing EEA charges in over 80% of cases involving defendants with Asian names. In contrast, the DOJ issued press releases in only half (51%) of EEA cases involving defendants with Western names [7].

Based on public evidence and convictions, it is undeniable that IP theft benefiting the PRC occurs and some are directed by individuals affiliated with the PRC government. But what seemed unclear to me was the scale of the alleged IP theft, since from our EEA research, it was evident that even with heightened scrutiny by the US government, less than half of the EEA cases were alleged theft for the benefit of China. Americans are outraged by economic espionage by any foreign country, friend or foe, but in particular by the scale and magnitude of the alleged theft by the PRC. As I delved into the origin of the $600 billion number, I found that no one who swore by the validity of the number could answer the simple question of where it came from. Finally, after much prodding, I was told in a meeting with a leading think tank to seek out Mark Cohen, a scholar who focuses on IP in Asia. Mark Cohen is the Asia IP Project Director at the Berkeley Center for Law & Technology. Before his academic career, Mark had worked at the American Embassy in Beijing on IP rights protection for American firms. He was, as he proudly pointed out, for a good number of years, America's point person on the ground protecting American IP.

Mark chuckled when I brought up the $600 billion number. He had looked carefully into the origin of the number, and it turns out that the number is derived from a rough, top-down estimate by the Organization for Economic Co-Operation and Development (OECD), of potential IP loss based on a percentage of national GDP. OECD estimated that 1–3% of a country's annual economic output may be forfeited due to IP loss, and as the US economy is around $23 trillion, the total IP loss annually may be in the range of $225-$600 billion. But what is IP loss and why is that loss completely ascribed to the PRC? IP loss is typically broken down into three categories: counterfeit goods, pirated software, and IP theft. IP theft is the act of illegally taking or using someone's intellectual property, or as the media popularly portrays it: stealing or repurposing someone else's innovative and leading-edge technology. As one can imagine, IP theft is a much smaller percentage of overall IP loss, and overall IP loss involves domestic as well as international bad actors. The whole $600 billion is entirely attributed to the PRC based on US customs seizure data for counterfeit goods, whose Chinese seizures comprise the majority of seizures but are primarily apparel, watches, and footwear [8]. In defense of the $600 billion number, scholars whom I have spoken to uniformly admit that arriving at an accurate number on IP theft is incredibly difficult, as by definition IP theft is conducted in secrecy and even when perpetrators are caught, the damages are difficult to assess. A top-down estimate is reasonable when bottoms up calculations are difficult to arrive at. Yet it seems to make no sense to take a rough estimate of overall IP loss and equate it with the much smaller subcategory of IP theft, and then attribute the whole number to one particular country.

Mark noted that since its original estimate, the OECD has further reduced the 1–3% range to 1.95% [9] as a more accurate barometer of annual IP loss. So how much IP theft by the PRC does occur annually? Mark's estimate is around 10% of the official range, so $25–60 billion annually. The US International Trade Commission (USITC), an agency of the US government, conducted a survey in 2009 of 5000 US firms in IP intensive parts of the US economy and based on survey information, estimated that US IP intensive firms' losses from IP infringements in China to be approximately $48 billion [10]. Corroborative research done by the Mercatus Institute at George Mason University suggest that that range is more realistic [11].

As Mark and others seem to be in the minority, I reached out to and connected with Roy Kamphausen, President of the National Bureau of Asian Research (NBR), whose institute published the most authoritative and most often quoted "*Report on the Theft of American Intellectual Property*." The Commission on the Theft of American Intellectual Property is an independent and bipartisan initiative including leading Americans such as Admiral Dennis Blair, former Director of National Intelligence and Jon Huntsman Jr., former Ambassador to China. The IP Commission released its original report in 2013, an update in 2017, as well as policy recommendations and reviews in 2018, 2019, and 2021 [12]. Roy was exceedingly cordial, but when I pressed him on the methodology by which the $600 billion number was arrived at, he could not answer my questions. Finally, he declared that NBR had believed that the threat from the PRC was real and urgent and that at the time of the report's first release, nobody in Washington D.C. was paying attention. The number had to be large enough to raise alarm in the nation's capital.

I decided to bring up my queries with the Department of Justice since the department is charged with prosecuting economic espionage acts. When I introduced our research findings to the National Security Division (NSD)—the unit within the DoJ charged with combating terrorism, espionage, cybercrime, foreign malign influence, and other threats to national security—I was told that economic espionage cases are exceedingly difficult to prosecute and convict. Therefore, if the government has intelligence of IP theft, it may convict on lesser crimes. This turns out to be the exact recipe for the China Initiative. In claiming that the

China Initiative was focused on stopping IP theft from China, the Department of Justice charged dozens of researchers, primarily Americans of Chinese descent, and presented them as agents and spies of the PRC. An examination of the China Initiative cases by the MIT Technology Review showed that actual charges raised by the government were on nondisclosure (e.g., for not stating an involvement with a Chinese university on Federal grant applications), wire fraud (e.g., for not reporting bank accounts or salaries in China), and making false statements. Yet even most of these cases fell apart based on misleading evidence and shoddy investigative work [13]. In sum, it is difficult not to conclude that the $600 billion number is simply inaccurate and grossly inflated at best. As someone who has worked in the high technology industry and been personally affected, I firmly believe that any dollar lost to IP theft is significant, but there is a real difference—namely 92%—between $48 billion and $600 billion. The evidence does not suggest anything to the magnitude that the government is presenting.

FBI Director Christopher Wray had publicly stated on numerous occasions that IP theft from the PRC is state sponsored [14]. In his 2020 speech at the Hudson Institute he asserted that, "China—the Chinese Communist Party—believes it is in a generational fight to surpass our country in economic and technological leadership." Numerous examples are given [4]. As a result, "We've now reached the point where the FBI is opening a new China-related counterintelligence case about every 10 h. Of the nearly 5000 active FBI counterintelligence cases currently underway across the country, almost half are related to China... We're conducting these kinds of investigations in all 56 of our field offices. And over the past decade, we've seen economic espionage cases with a link to China increase by approximately 1300%." The most galling is cybertheft of IP. In 2015, President Obama publicly asked President Xi to agree "that neither the US nor the Chinese government will conduct or knowingly support cyber-enabled theft of intellectual property, including trade secrets or other confidential business information for commercial advantage [15]." However, the US continues to uncover and file charges against state actors in China for alleged cyberthefts. For example, in 2021, the Department of Justice charged four nationals and residents of the PRC with a campaign to hack into the computer systems of dozens of victim companies, universities, and government entities in the US and abroad between 2011 and 2018. The indictment alleged that three of the four defendants were officers in the Hainan State Security Department

(HSSD), a provincial arm of the PRC's Ministry of State Security [16]. Because these and other defendants are based in China, they are almost never brought to trial in the US and proven guilty beyond a reasonable doubt. The Center for Strategic and International Studies estimates the cost of cybertheft by the PRC to be around $20–30 billion annually [17].

The FBI makes a further argument for state sponsored IP theft through PRC's forced IP transfer, which is PRC government mandated IP transfer from foreign companies to Chinese firms in exchange for market access or business licenses in China. Most American firms manage the exchange by transferring last generation technologies to Chinese joint ventures or designated partners. For 4 years I represented Intel Corporation laboring on this exact topic, negotiating with the PRC government on transfer of a last generation wireless technology in exchange for collaboration on next-generation wireless standards and spectrum allocation in China. An oft cited example is General Motors' investments in China. In 1997, in order to setup facilities in China, GM was required by the PRC government to form a joint venture with SAIC Motors that involved technology transfer. Committee of 100 co-founder Shirley Young, who was Vice President at GM at the time, was instrumental in shepherding the joint venture. As early as 2003, China became GM's second largest single market. By 2018, GM delivered more than 3.64 million vehicles in China [18]. In 2018, Tesla became the first foreign automotive maker to setup a facility in China without a joint venture partner or technology transfer requirement. In 2023, Tesla accounted for 13.2% of the EV market in China [19]. Experts whom I have spoken to all agree that while the practice must be vigorously contested by the US government, it is a transaction between two willing parties. The foreign company willingly enters into an IP transfer in exchange for access to the burgeoning Chinese market. The potential for IP loss is real, but the potential for profit gain is real as well.

The FBI finally points to the Thousand Talent Program (TTP), which is a PRC government sponsored program to entice scientists globally to work in China. All successful applicants receive a starting bonus of 1 million yuan (US $151,000) as well as the opportunity to apply for research funding of 3–5 million yuan [20]. As the FBI states on its website on "The China Threat," Chinese Talent Plans encourage trade secret theft and economic espionage [21]. In my exchanges with the CATO institute, a libertarian think tank, I was provided copies of internal FBI documents on the TTP acquired through CATO's Freedom of Information Act (FOIA) requests. The FBI documents admit that talent programs by their nature are not illegal, but raise serious concerns about the PRC's implementation of the TTP. There is real and substantiated concern that certain US researchers have not reported earnings drawn from the TTP or have taken proprietary IP to China as part of the Program [22]. In 2022, Xiaorong You of Lansing, Michigan was sentenced to serve 168 months in prison for conspiracy to commit trade secret theft and economic espionage, among other charges. You was convicted of stealing valuable trade secrets related to the formulation of coatings for the inside of beverage cans and attempting to set up a competing firm in China, with grants from the PRC government including the TTP [23].

I spoke to David Zweig, Distinguished Visiting Professor in the Taipei School of Economics and Political Science at National Tsinghua University in Taiwan, who specializes in the long history of China struggling with its talent brain drain. Talent brain drain has been a severe problem for China. 70% of Chinese overseas students never return to China. Since 1978, only 275,000 students out of 1,060,000 overseas Chinese students returned home [24]. David was kind enough to share a draft of a book titled "The War for Chinese Talent in America" that he's been working on that details the long history of talent loss and government responses in China. Specific to the Thousand Talents Program, David has tracked around 500 of the estimated 1500 scientists and engineers recruited under the TTP, and found that the vast majority of TTP grantees are academics and TTP grants university research focused, the results of which are published in public journals [25]. David echoed other experts whom I had spoken to by noting that regrettably, US–China scientific collaboration, oftentimes facilitated by Chinese American scientists, has become the focal point of US government investigations into IP theft by the PRC.

Chris Marquis is a Professor of Chinese Management at Cambridge University. Previously, he was a Professor in Sustainable Global Enterprise at Cornell University and before that spent over 11 years as a professor at Harvard. I had gotten to know Chris well during my time at the Committee of 100 and Chris was willing to share his experiences as a recipient of a TPP grant. From his research and teaching in China, he became acquainted with the faculty at the University of Electronic Science and Technology of China (UESTC) in Chengdu, China. UESTC is known as one of the best technical universities in China and has close ties with the Chinese defense industry and its nuclear weapons program.

When Chris visited the campus, there were parts he was prohibited from because of military work there.

In Chris' recounting, the TTP application process was quite involved. It took him more work to prepare than the arduous academic tenure process he had experienced. He had to assemble copies of his entire academic output, awards, degrees, and other materials. Importantly, he had to write a proposal for what kind of work he would do if given a TTP grant. He proposed establishing a research center on business social responsibility which could hold conferences and events as well as executive and research workshops. Through UESTC, the Chinese Education Ministry approved the award and in 2017 Chris established a research center funded with a 3M RMB ($400,000) grant.

Chris recounted fondly his directing the UESTC center. Before COVID-19, he spent 1–2 months a year in Chengdu, a city famous for its relaxed attitude and spicy cuisine. The center held a number of annual events on sustainability in businesses, some geared towards academics and others towards practitioners. Chris saw value not just for the Chinese participants, but more so for international visitors. This included scholars from around the world comprising the US, Europe, Hong Kong, and Singapore who were able to meet and engage with their Chinese counterparts and see what was happening on the ground.

Chris lamented that critics of the TTP blunder the fact that global academic exchanges are characteristic of all universities around the world, and benefit all parties. He emphasized that if an American researcher is conducting work on national security or other export-controlled areas, he should not be involved. However, in his experience, the majority of exchanges do not involve access to restricted information and are around general knowledge sharing. Through the TPP, Chris met many other Western scholars, some recruited for shorter commitments of 2 months per year, while others for longer commitments of 9 months per year. One highlight was an annual event held at the Great Hall of the People near Tiananmen Square, at which former Chinese Premier Li Keqiang and his staff engaged with the "foreign experts" about recommendations they had for China's development. In 2018 and 2020, Chris presented on the importance of entrepreneurship for areas such as environmental protection and poverty reduction.

Under President Trump, UESTC was placed on the US Department of Commerce's Entity List, which means that US businesses can no longer trade with it. Soon after, Chris received a call from Cornell's legal counsel.

At the time, there was significant negative press coverage of the TTP and explosive details about FBI detentions of Americans recruited to the program. The attorney was friendly and wanted to know what Chris' work consisted of. Chris was told that UESTC was now on the Entity List so he should never transfer any Cornell resources to UESTC. Specifically, even something as small as a pen, if it is from Cornell, he cannot give to anyone at UESTC. The reaction of his UESTR counterpart was equally intriguing. Chris got a WeChat message from UESTC's HR director. He was given a list of every mention on the Internet of his involvement with the TTP and told to have them removed. The HR director told Chris this was done to help him given the crackdown by the US authorities. Chris was later told that the TPP would continue but under the new name of National High-end Foreign Experts Recruitment Plan. Chris' TPP contract was for 5 years, and it expired in 2022. For all of China's perceived capacity to discern and steal American IP, Chris observed that the TPP was notorious for canceling contracts with outstanding Western scholars, including with Philip Dybvig, shortly before he won the Nobel Prize in Economics in 2022.

Cybertheft is incredibly difficult to detect and prevent, and almost impossible to bring foreign perpetrators to justice. IP transfer is a transaction between two willing parties occurring under Chinese jurisdiction and jurisprudence. While it is true that the US government does not condition access to the American market on IP transfer and as such the PRC is creating an "uneven playing field" for American companies in China, American companies enter into such IP transfers fully aware of the consequences. US–China scientific collaboration, on the other hand, is open and public, and participating American academics reside in America. When an American academic is invited to join the Thousand Talents Program, as David noted, the majority of them prefer to live in the US with periodic visits to China. As the assumption in Washington D.C. hardened to $600 billion worth of advanced IP stolen annually by the PRC, the scale and magnitude of the number begged the existence of a massive espionage ring. With US–China scientific collaboration public and trackable, thousands of American academics—most of them Chinese Americans—who for the last several decades were actively encouraged by American universities to conduct research and partnerships with China, naturally fell under suspicion. This explains the sudden explosion in FBI investigations related to the PRC as publicly stated by the FBI director.

Since normalization in 1978, the US and PRC have accelerated scientific collaboration across a variety of areas, often through academic institutions and university laboratories. In the Nature Index, which tracks output in 82 selected natural science journals, the two nations are each other's most important collaborative partners. Between 2015 and 2020, the number of papers co-authored by China and the US leapt from 3412 to 5213—more than any other country pairing in the Index [26]. Research by Jenny Lee, Professor of Higher Education at Arizona University, showed that the US benefits just as much, if not more, from collaboration with China. A scientometric study of Scopus co-publications—a comprehensive database that indexes peer-reviewed literature—over the past 5 years showed a continuous rise in bilateral collaboration between the two countries. The study demonstrated ways in which China played a leading role in US–China research collaboration, based on first authorship and governmental funding patterns. It showed that from 2018 to 2023, US research article publications would have declined without co-authorship with China, whereas China's publication rate would have risen without the US [27].

JASON is an independent scientific advisory board established in 1960 that comprises the most illustrious American scientists who consult with the US government on matters of defense science and technology. In 2019, the group was tasked by the National Science Foundation to produce a report on Fundamental Research Security in response to perceived IP theft by the PRC. The report concluded that, "many of the problems of foreign influence that have been identified are ones that can be addressed within the framework of research integrity, and that the benefits of openness in research and of the inclusion of talented foreign researchers dictate against measures that would wall off particular areas of fundamental research. We expect that a reinvigorated commitment to US standards of research integrity and the tradition of open science by all stakeholders will drive continued preeminence of the United States in science, engineering, and technology by attracting and retaining the world's best talent [28]."

On March 21, 2024, the National Science Foundation (NSF) released a new report by JASON, titled "Safeguarding the Research Enterprise." This report builds upon the 2019 Fundamental Research Security report. In this study, JASON was tasked to comment on specific steps NSF might take to identify sensitive areas of research and describe processes to address security in those areas. The report presented eight key findings and six recommendations. It emphasized the importance of international collaboration in research while acknowledging various risks and the necessity to distinguish between sensitive and nonsensitive research. It advised against broadly designating scientific fields as sensitive and recommended assessing project sensitivity case by case. It also cautioned against expanding export controls to include fundamental research areas, warning of increased research costs, talent pipeline reduction, and hindrance to broader US economic and national security interests [29]. The assumption that IP theft by the PRC may be state sponsored is not without merit, but the wholehearted focus on US–China scientific collaboration is misguided and as subsequent data and public cases illustrate, severely detrimental to American values and competitiveness.

The FBI declares that IP theft by the PRC is a whole of society attack [30]. Speaking before the Senate Intelligence Committee in 2018, FBI Director Wray remarked that, "one of the things we're trying to do is view the China threat as not just a whole-of-government threat, but a whole-of-society threat on their end." Unfortunately, in practice this means that anyone who is Chinese—a student, a businessperson, a researcher, a tourist, or simply an ethnic Chinese—can be viewed as an agent or spy. Many Americans have heard of "driving while black," but most of them have yet to hear about "researching while Chinese [31]." The Committee of 100 study on the Economic Espionage Act found that 27% of presumed Asian Americans charged under the EEA were not convicted of any crimes. An additional 6% of Asian Americans were convicted only of process offenses like false statements. In total, 1 in 3 Asian Americans accused of espionage may have been falsely accused. Half of the defendants with Western names (49%) convicted under the EEA were given sentences of probation only, with no incarceration. In contrast, the vast majority of defendants of Asian descent (75%) were sent to prison, in particular defendants of Chinese descent (80%). In addition, Chinese and Asian defendants convicted of economic espionage received average sentences of 27 and 23 months respectively, roughly twice as long as the average sentence of 12 months for defendants with Western names. Although movies and TV dramas inevitably highlight the "perp walk," only 38% of EEA defendants with Western names were actually arrested and handcuffed. Instead, most defendants with Western names received a formal letter summoning them to court to face the charges against them. In contrast, the first time 69% of defendants of Asian descent and 78%

of defendants of Chinese descent learned that they had been charged was when they were arrested, generally with handcuffs [32].

As President of the Committee of 100, I had the privilege to work with many Chinese American scientists, who against all odds, decided to speak out and pursue justice for themselves and others. Their cases illustrate how when our assumptions are wrong, real lives are ruined. Sherry Chen was a hydrologist with the National Weather Service inside the Commerce Department. In 2011, she received the Larry R. Johnson Special Award for producing lifesaving river forecasts. In 2014, as Sherry was entering her work building, she was arrested by six FBI agents and charged with unlawfully downloading sensitive government data and acting as a spy for China. She faced penalties of 25 years in prison and $1 million in fines. In 2015, less than a week before the trial was scheduled to begin, the government announced that it was dismissing all charges. Yet the Commerce Department would not let her return to work. In 2016, the Commerce Department terminated her employment despite her acquittal. Instead of fading into the wind, Sherry appealed to the Merit Systems Protection Board. After a full hearing, the judge rejected the agency's allegations and ordered the Commerce Department to immediately reinstate her employment. Through the process, it was discovered that inside the Commerce Department, there existed a rogue unit, the Investigations and Threat Management Service (ITMS), that had targeted thousands of federal employees based on race and national origin, Sherry Chen being one of the victims.

A review in 2021 by the US Senate Committee on Commerce, Science, & Transportation produced a committee investigation report on "the Abuse and Misconduct at the Commerce Department [33]." Among the report's findings were that "investigating threats against the Secretary of Commerce and the Department's assets without a clearly defined mission ultimately led to the mutation of the ITMS into a rogue, unaccountable police force across multiple presidential administrations." "The ITMS searched Department servers and monitored employee email accounts to scan for evidence of foreign influence as early as 2014. These searches began focusing on an operation to uncover connections between Department employees and actors within the PRC government. To achieve this end, the ITMS targeted departmental divisions with comparably high proportions of Asian American employees."

In 2019, Sherry filed a federal lawsuit against the United States, seeking accountability for the government's misconduct. In 2022, she reached a historic settlement. The settlement, one of the largest ever paid to an individual plaintiff in Commerce Department history, included compensation valued at approximately $1.8 million. I spoke with Sherry when I first joined the Committee of 100. By then, she had already marched for more than 6 years on her long and harrowing journey for justice, with no end in sight. I asked her why she was continuing to speak up and spending costly sums which she did not have, in an uncertain legal pursuit against the US government. Sherry replied that she wasn't doing it for herself, but rather for all others who might have been unjustly prosecuted simply because of their ethnicity or national origin. Her courage took me by surprise. For a very long time, our community's general stance is to keep our heads down and do good work. In a 1966 New York Times article titled "Success Story, Japanese American Style," sociologist William Petersen first coined the term "model minority" to praise Japanese Americans for "enduring the most discrimination and worst injustices," and achieving success in America "by their own almost totally unaided efforts." Sherry was breaking down that model minority myth. Her case helped to shed light on how the assumption of anyone who looks Chinese may be suspect of being a spy for the PRC, has led to systemic abuse of individual liberties and rights in America.

In September 2022, I sat in a courtroom for the United States Court of Appeals for the Third Circuit in Philadelphia as the judge heard Professor Xiaoxing Xi's arguments for suing the Federal Bureau of Investigation. In May 2023, the judge decided that Xiaoxing may bring forward his case against the US government for wrongful prosecution and violating his family's constitutional rights by engaging in unlawful search, seizure, and surveillance [34]. The decision was monumental because appropriately, the FBI is well protected against lawsuits since as a nation, we don't want FBI agents to worry about legal ramifications in conducting their lawful duties. Only in extraordinary cases of malfeasance or gross misconduct would a judge allow a case to go forward. Xiaoxing's is one of such cases.

When I first sat down with Xiaoxing he poured out his travails. As Chair of the Physics Department at Temple University, he was a well-respected scientist. One morning in 2015, he was woken up by thunderous pounding on his door, and when he went to look, FBI agents swarmed in, arrested him in front of his wife and young children, and led him away in handcuffs. Later he found out that he was charged with sharing sensitive technology with scientists in China, with fines up to $1 million and 80 years in prison. As Xiaoxing described to me, as soon as the FBI agent mentioned the technology, called a pocket heater, he knew immediately it was a mistake. In fact, after leading experts in the field provided sworn affidavits that any communications that Xiaoxing may have had with scientists in China involved nonproprietary technologies, the FBI dropped its case. What motivated Xiaoxing to pursue justice was that during the pre-trial process it was discovered that the FBI agent in charge actually spoke to the inventor of the pocket heater and was told that the technology was "widely known" and not "revolutionary." Yet the FBI agent hid such information and knowingly went ahead with the arrest and prosecution. In his testimony to a Congressional Roundtable entitled "Researching while Chinese American: Ethnic Profiling, Chinese American Scientists and a New American Brain Drain," hosted by Representative Jamie Raskin, Chair of the Oversight Subcommittee on Civil Rights and Civil Liberties, and Representative Judy Chu, Chair of the Congressional Asian Pacific American Caucus (CAPAC), Xiaoxing uttered the following: People have asked me, "How can the Department of Justice avoid wrongly accusing innocent people like they did in your case?" My answer is that they can't unless they stop considering Chinese professors, scientists, and students as nontraditional collectors, or spies, for China.

In 2022, Professor Gang Chen of MIT, along with a team of leading scientists, announced a major scientific discovery of a material that could be the best semiconductor material ever found [35]. Yet just a short year before, I had worked with him on his case after his arrest as a spy for China. In 2021, the Department of Justice arrested Gang for allegedly concealing his activities with the PRC and pocketing vast sums from China. 170 MIT professors co-wrote a letter to the MIT president refuting point by point the government's allegations [36]. The US government alleged that "since 2013 Chen and his research group has received approximately $29 million of foreign funding, including $19 million from the PRC's Southern University of Science and Technology." The fact was that MIT was the recipient of this money, and Gang was appointed by the university to negotiate on MIT's behalf. The US government alleged that "Chen hid his affiliation and collaborations with China in applying and reporting on a Department of Energy grant and in doing so committed "wire fraud," a federal felony." The fact was that Chen's CV, available for download on MIT's website, contains 62 references to China, and his publications cite international funding specifically from the very sources claimed in the complaint to be "hidden." The letter ended with the simple phrase, "We are all Gang Chen." Across the nation, thousands of professors signed on to their school's petition ending with "We are all Gang Chen." Initiated at Stanford University, scholars from more than 200 schools joined in their calls to end the China Initiative [37]. The government dropped its case in 2022.

After his acquittal, I sat down for coffee with Gang in Boston, and he talked about his harrowing ordeal and how it radically upended his life. He had never before thought about politics or law. He was lucky that MIT funded his legal defense. So many other professors, when accused by the FBI, were immediately suspended or terminated by their universities before any trial had even begun. Left to their own devices, the process of retaining a lawyer and mounting a defense against the government can amount to hundreds of thousands if not millions of dollars. Many had to mortgage their homes and borrow from friends and family. Even when their cases are dropped, like Gang's, there is seldom an explanation or even a word of apology for lives turned upside down. Besides FBI led investigations, National Institutes of Health (NIH) inquiries have led to hundreds of American scientists, most of them Chinese American tenured professors, to lose their jobs. Science chronicled the lack of due process, transparency, and devastation on scientist lives in an article titled "Pall of Suspicion: The National Institutes of Health's 'China Initiative' has upended Hundreds of Lives and Destroyed Scores of Academic Careers [38]." On July 10, 2024, Dr. Jane Y. Wu, a prominent Chinese American researcher inn neurology and genetics at Northwestern University's Feinberg School of Medicine, took her own life, after her lab was shut down amidst NIH investigations. "The investigations killed her career," said Dr. Xiao-Fan Wang, a distinguished professor in cancer research at Duke University, "She was such a devoted scientist. Denying her the right to do research was like taking away the most important thing in her life." Dr. Wu was buried in Chicago on July 17. She was 60 years old [39].

NIH is by far the largest funder of academic biomedical research in the US. The Science article quotes David Brenner, who was vice chancellor for health sciences at the University of California, San Diego, saying that "if NIH says there's a conflict, then there's a conflict, because NIH is always right." Academic institutions, when faced with the possibility of losing millions in federal funding, typically go the route of speedy dismissal or forced retirement of accused scientists. On August 15, 2024, NIH Director Dr. Monica Bertagnolli acknowledged that the government's actions had "unintended consequences" for these communities, leading them to feel "targeted and alienated." Gang told me that because of his scientific pedigree, he had multiple offers from leading universities around the world. He chose to stay in Boston because it is where his children were born and where home is. But he vowed never to take federal funding again.

In 2021, working with the University of Arizona, the Committee of 100 conducted a survey of 1949 scientists around the US [40]. Titled "Racial Profiling Among Scientists of Chinese Descent and Consequences for the U.S. Scientific Community," survey results show a consistent pattern of racial profiling, as perceived by Chinese scientists. The costs include a negative impact on scientists' research projects, a greater reluctance to pursue federal grants, and considerations to leave the US. Survey data showed a wave of fear among scientists of non-Chinese descent as well, in which scientists have described cutting ties with their collaborators in China, no longer hiring Chinese postdocs, and limiting communications with scholars in China, even at the expense of their own research projects. 42.2% of scientists of Chinese descent feel racially profiled by the US government, while only 8.6% of scientists of non-Chinese descent feel so. 38.4% of scientists of Chinese descent experience more difficulty in obtaining funding for research projects as a result of their race, ethnicity, and country of origin, compared to only 14.2% of scientists of non-Chinese descent. 50.7% of scientists of Chinese descent feel considerable fear and/or anxiety that they are being surveilled by the US government, compared to only 11.7% of scientists of non-Chinese descent. Among non-US citizen scientists in the sample, 42.1% of scientists of Chinese descent indicate that the FBI investigations affected their plans to stay in the U.S., while only 7.1% of scientists of non-Chinese descent report so. Other findings report the same worrying trend of talent brain drain [41]. A 2023 research paper found that since 2018, "scientists of Chinese descent in the United States now face higher incentives to leave the United States and lower incentives to apply for federal grants [42]." In 2022, the Wall Street Journal reported on the outflow of thousands of Chinese scientists from the US [43]. But perhaps this is all necessary collateral damage in the existential struggle between the US and PRC? How much worse off are we if some Chinese American scientists or engineers left the US?

Between 2011 and 2020, nine companies featured in the Fortune 500 ranking were founded or co-founded by Chinese Americans. At their peak, these companies combined to support 332,000 jobs and their market capitalization amounted to $1.5 trillion in today's value after adjusting for inflation. One such trailblazer was David Lam, who started Lam Research—a semiconductor equipment designer and manufacturer—in 1980, and later became the first Chinese American entrepreneur to take a company public on the NASDAQ. Under Lam's leadership, the company introduced the first fully automated plasma etching system for semiconductor manufacturing, allowing for the rapid miniaturization of semiconductor wafers, crucial for the development of the personal computer. Lam's automated production processes greatly contributed to the emergence of the US as a global leader in semiconductor manufacturing. In 2018, Lam Research was the second largest semiconductor manufacturer in the Greater Bay Area, employing over 3000 people. Inspired by role models like David Lam, an increasing number of Chinese Americans have opted for entrepreneurship. Between 1980 and 1984, 9% of high tech startups in Silicon Valley were run by people of Chinese heritage, mostly first-generation immigrants; this percentage more than doubled, to 20%, in 1995–1998. In 1998, Chinese American led enterprises collectively made over US$13.2 billion in sales and created nearly 42,000 jobs in Silicon Valley [44]. In the area of semiconductor chipset technology, an area of pivotal competition between the US and PRC, some of the most valuable American companies have been founded or run by Chinese Americans. This includes Nvidia, the most valuable artificial intelligence chipset company in the world (Jensen Huang, co-founder and President), AMD and Intel, the leading microprocessor companies in the world (Lisa Su, CEO and Lip-Bu Tan, CEO), Broadcom, the pioneering wireless and broadband chipset company (Hock Tan, CEO), among many others.

The three assumptions on IP theft by the PRC are not only mistaken, but are grossly counterproductive to American values and interests. First, they obscure the fact that while IP theft by the PRC is a real and pressing concern, the long-term challenge to American innovative leadership is our ability to attract and retain global talent. Second, they mask the reality that many Chinese firms are innovative and fast becoming US technology peers. Take the example of Huawei. Huawei has been pilloried in the US for being a tool of the PRC government. While I cannot speak to the national security risk that Huawei poses, judging from personal interactions and conversations with industry insiders, the company is a true technology powerhouse. I remember visiting Huawei for the first time in 2005 and meeting with the then CEO. It was clear that the company cared deeply about research and development and invested heavily in innovation. I was told about cots on the office floor so engineers could work through the night to solve an engineering problem. There are real technology reasons why Huawei became the world's largest telecom equipment provider, and before the Trump sanctions crippled its smartphone business, the world's largest smartphone provider. Similarly, Huawei had 25% of the US rural wireless business because it was affordable and good [45]. I remember speaking to the former CTO of Sprint Corporation (before its merger with T-Mobile) and asking for his opinion on Huawei's technology. His answer was that it was good and getting better. Despite US sanctions that limit Huawei's ability to source components for its phones and other gadgets, the company projected growth of 9% for 2023. In 2023, Huawei also launched its premium Mate 60 Pro smartphone that used all domestic chip technologies [46]. The overwhelming and exclusive focus on IP theft takes the focus off our real challenge, which is innovative Chinese firms that American companies must take note of and train their attention to. Third, they hurt our values. Racial profiling is simply against American values. To be clear, there are real national security threats posed by foreign state actors, including the PRC. IP theft, cybertheft, and economic espionage are real concerns that merit serious attention. The challenge lies in ensuring that our responses are narrowly tailored, evidence-based, and uphold civil liberties. Overly broad policies—

such as the profiling of Chinese American scientists—undermine our democratic values and alienate the very communities that are essential to our innovative, defense, and cultural competitiveness.

When policies are implemented through the lens of fear rather than fact, they corrode the very ways of life they seek to defend. The damage is not just to individuals, but to the system as a whole—one that thrives on openness, diversity, and global collaboration.

Better assumptions can be:

Assumption 1: Chinese Firms are Becoming Worthy Technology Competitors

Assumption 2: To Compete Against the PRC, we Must Double Down on our Ability to Attract and Retain the World's Best Talents

Assumption 3: To Combat IP Theft, we Must Foster Active Collaboration among Government Agencies, Corporations, Universities, and Affected Communities

Today, I still hear many friends who casually remark, "oh that product is cheap, it must be made in China." They are correct, but only partially. Many products that are cheap are made in China. But increasingly, expensive and innovative products are being made in China as well. Take Electric Vehicles (EV). More EVs were sold in China in 2022 than the rest of the world combined. China has become the world's largest automobile exporter because of EVs [47]. The Chinese innovated across the entire EV supply chain and dominate in lithium iron phosphate batteries, as well as other emerging battery technologies. Chinese automakers are around 30% quicker in development than legacy manufacturers, largely because they have upended global practices built around decades of making complex combustion engine cars. They work on many stages of development at once. They are willing to substitute traditional suppliers for smaller, faster ones. They run more virtual tests instead of time-consuming mechanical ones. And they are redefining when a car is ready to sell on the market [48]. Global EV sales surged in May 2025, hitting 1.6 million units sold. That brings the total for the year to date to 7.2 million EVs, a 28% increase compared to the same period in 2024. The big winner: China. The country sold a record-breaking 1 million EVs in May 2025 alone. That's a 33% jump year-over-year, and a 10% increase compared to April. The rest of the world saw solid gains too, but North America lagged far behind [49].

According to the International Energy Agency, Chinese companies like BYD, SAIC, and Geely produce 70% of the electric cars sold globally in 2024. Automakers in the US produced just 5%. One in five new cars sold worldwide is electric, and the percentage is increasing. The Big and Beautiful Bill passed by President Trump in July 2025 eliminated tax credits of up to $7500 for electric vehicle buyers, clawed back money for fast chargers, and phased out subsidies for companies that set up battery factories and lithium mines. Yet even in the US, electric and hybrid vehicles will eventually displace gasoline powered vehicles. Sales of cars that run solely on fossil fuels have been declining for a decade, accounting for less than 74% of the US market in 2025 [50]. In the beginning of the 1970s, the Detroit Big Three had 85% of the American automotive market, and "Made in Japan" was considered cheap and easily ignored [51]. Decades of market share drops, plant closings and job losses, mergers and acquisitions, and government bailouts later, today GM, Ford, and Chrysler survive but are way behind in the EV race. Companies fall behind when they believe too much in their own infallibility and underestimate the competition. Nations do as well.

From Shein and Temu, favorite fast fashion retailers for Generation Z, to Tik Tok, used by 41% of Americans, Chinese companies are demonstrating a level of technology sophistication embraced by Americans and beyond. Decades ago, Americans studied the Japanese to learn how they produced high quality products at lower cost and faster turnaround time. Not enough work today is being done to study how Chinese companies are increasingly producing high quality products at lower costs and faster turnaround time. Our better assumption should be that independent of IP theft, Chinese companies across multiple industries are becoming technologically savvy and worthy competitors. We must pay heed and study our competition, and not delude ourselves into thinking that we in America have a monopoly on innovation. Part of the underestimation can be traced to the assumption that the Chinese are somehow less innovative because of their political system. I vividly recall meeting a former China Director at the National Security Council, who is also an acclaimed scholar on China. He declared that the Chinese are good traders but not good innovators. He made the observation because he and many other scholars believe that an authoritarian regime will necessarily hinder innovation and creativity. If there is no political or social freedom, how can people have the mental space to innovate and create? I don't know if this theoretical equivalence between political freedom and technological innovation holds true in the long run, but past decades have clearly illustrated that Chinese entrepreneurs and scientists are highly innovative and adaptive, despite the limitations of their political system.

When I first joined Intel, I worked under legendary CEO Andy Grove, himself a refugee from Hungary. Andy had a saying that I will always treasure, "my greatest assets walk in the door every morning at 9am and walk out the door every night at 6pm." In the competition for innovation leadership, the real IP that America must protect and retain is our diverse talent pool, drawn from domestic but crucially from international destinations, including from China. There's a reason why Elon Musk, born in South Africa, or Sergey Brin, born in Russia, decided to make America the home of Tesla and Google. Similarly, we must protect and retain the reasons why Jerry Yang, born in Taiwan, or Eric Yuan, born in mainland China, made America the home of Yahoo! and Zoom. The National Science Board found that in 2016, the US awarded nearly

800,000 science and engineering first university degrees, broadly equivalent to a bachelor's degree. In the meantime, China produced 1.7 million science and engineering first university degrees. In 2016, the US awarded about 40,000 science and engineering doctorates while in 2015, China awarded about 34,000 science and engineering doctoral degrees. In the US, a substantial proportion of science and engineering doctoral degrees are conferred to international students with temporary visas. In 2017, temporary visa holders earned one-third (34%) of science and engineering doctoral degrees, a relatively stable proportion over time. In particular, they account for half or more of the doctoral degrees awarded in engineering, mathematics and computer sciences, and economics. Three Asian countries—China, India, and South Korea—are the largest source countries and accounted for just over half (54%) of all international recipients of US science and engineering research doctoral degrees since 2000. A majority of the science and engineering doctorate recipients with temporary visas—ranging between 64 and 71% between 2003 and 2017—stayed in the US 5 years after obtaining their degree. Those from China and India, however, saw a decline in their respective "stay rates" from 93 and 90%, respectively, in 2003 to 84% and 85%, respectively, in 2013. The US is still the largest destination for international students worldwide (19% in 2016), but enrollment of international students at US institutions has declined since 2016 [52].

In March 2025, the House Select Committee on China sent a letter to the Presidents of Carnegie Mellon, Purdue University, Stanford University, the University of Illinois, the University of Maryland, and the University of Southern California requesting information on each of their policies and practices regarding the enrollment of Chinese students in advanced STEM programs, questioning their involvement in federally funded research [53]. In May 2025, the State Department announced that "under President Trump's leadership, the US State Department will work with the Department of Homeland Security to aggressively revoke visas for Chinese students, including those with connections to the Chinese Communist Party or studying in critical fields [54]." Just weeks later, President Trump posted on his social media platform, Truth Social, that "our deal with China is done, subject to final approval with President Xi and me. Likewise, we will provide to China what was agreed to, including Chinese students using our colleges and universities (which has always been good with me!) [55]." But the damage is done. Chinese student enrollment in the US has fallen by more than 25%, from about

370,000 in 2019 to roughly 277,000 in the 2023–24 academic year, and according to all indications, will continue to decline given political uncertainties in the US [56].

The competition for talent rests on quantity and quality. The Chinese population of 1.4 billion is approximately four times the US population, and if each country were to produce a proportionate number of science and engineering graduates, the US must rely on international talent to maintain its quantitative edge. Qualitatively, many international students who come to study in the US are the cream of the crop in their home countries. I recall dining with Committee of 100 member Jerry Guo and learning about his life story. Jerry came to the US in 1987 to pursue his PhD in science and engineering, afterwards working for AT&T Bell Labs, and later founded a Nasdaq listed technology firm. Over salad and soup, Jerry casually mentioned that he was the top national examinations scholar in his province in China, a province of tens of millions of people. Jerry's example is one of many. America is and will be the pre-eminent leader in innovation if and only if we continue to attract and retain the world's best talents.

Even if IP theft from the PRC is much smaller than assumed, it is still significant and must be tackled effectively. At the Committee of 100, we worked with the White House Office of Science and Technology Policy (OSTP) to help standardize and streamline university disclosure guidelines so that American scientists understand their roles in a changing political climate. The OSTP has engaged with community stakeholders regarding the implementation of National Security Presidential Memorandum-33 (NSPM-33) on National Security Policy for United States Government Supported Research and Development [57]. The effort hopes to standardize and coordinate disparate federal agencies' research security policies. The slowdown and stoppage in US–China scientific collaboration may be hurting the US more as research suggests that the US tend to benefit more from US–China scientific collaboration [58]. Since government actions take time, universities such as MIT have released their own policies on engagement with China. MIT's report, titled "University Engagement with China, an MIT Approach," recommends combining selective engagement with targeted risk assessment and management. This approach is designed to help MIT advance knowledge and the needs of America, without damaging American national security or economy, without endangering human rights, and in ways that are consistent with MIT's core values [59].

To combat IP Theft, active dialog and collaboration must be fostered between the FBI and affected communities, including universities, corporations, and in particular the Chinese American community. At the Committee of 100, we commenced active outreach to the FBI, including FBI offices on the West and East Coasts. I wanted to understand why the FBI overwhelmingly focused on the Chinese American community. My understanding, in speaking with FBI agents and scholars who study the topic, is that the FBI's overwhelming focus generally derives from the following data points. The first, is that for the last four decades, across American universities, corporations, and industries, collaboration and exchange with China were actively encouraged. Chinese Americans, already trusted employees of American organizations and with the prerequisite cultural and linguistic capabilities, became natural interlocutors. Thus, when US government policies shifted from engagement to competition with the PRC, Chinese Americans became easily suspect. Second, the FBI cites President Xi's numerous public remarks on the role of overseas Chinese "in realizing the Chinese dream of national rejuvenation as they are patriotic and rich in capital, talent, resources and business connections [60]." To the FBI, these public statements, coupled with documented attempts by individuals associated with the PRC government to approach Chinese Americans, easily led to suspicions on *all* Chinese Americans. Third, FBI agents are driven by what senior management chooses to measure. When political leaders decry China and Chinese threats at every turn, FBI agents naturally do their best to comply with senior directives and focus on anything remotely having to do with "Chinese." While the FBI has made significant strides, ethnic and racial diversity at the bureau still falls far short of representative proportions in American society [61]. In terms of racial demographics, the FBI's workforce was 75% white in 2009 and 74.4% white in 2019. Additionally, whites held 79.5% of the top GS grade positions in 2009 and 77.6% in 2019 [62]. Without the prerequisite cultural understanding and sensitivity, innocent activities can easily be misconstrued as pernicious or dangerous. I still remember a former US attorney telling me how an FBI agent came to her with suspicions regarding a Chinese American scientist, who according to the agent, made curious trips to China every spring at irregular times. The US attorney asked if these trips were made during lunar new year celebrations, to which the agent replied, "what is that?".

At the Committee of 100, we hosted several off the record discussions between the FBI and Chinese American scientists from well-known universities on the West and East Coasts. I remember sitting in the middle of the conference table and hearing scientist after scientist talk about their despair in not being able to trust their government and lingering fear for simply doing their work. Purposefully, I asked two questions, one to the FBI delegation and the other to the scientists. To the FBI, I asked that while some media has insinuated that Chinese Americans are coerced by the PRC government to steal IP because of family ties in China, has the FBI found any documented truth to this. To which the FBI responded that there is evidence of incentives offered, but not of coercion. Turning to the scientists, I asked that if you were approached by any foreign government to commit a crime against the US, what would you do. The answer was to refuse and contact the FBI. But the present situation has made many of them afraid to contact the FBI. At the 2023 Committee of 100 annual conference and gala in San Jose, California, we held a panel titled, "Community Outreach with Local FBI: A Roundtable Discussion with Bay Area FBI and Asian American Leaders." Featured speakers included Jeff Fields, Assistant Special Agent in charge of the FBI's Counterintelligence Branch in San Francisco, Reuben Chen, Board Member, Monte Jade West Science and Technology Association, Fengmin Gong, Chairman, Hua Yuan Science and Technology Association, and Peter Michelson, Professor of Physics at Stanford. The conversation centered on addressing two key concerns: how to prevent US technology and intellectual property from being stolen, and how to mitigate and correct the counterproductive approach adopted by the US government in response.

Personally, I was invited by the FBI to attend the FBI Citizens Academy. The 8-week long course for community leaders helped me understand that post 9/11, the FBI has transformed itself to become a domestic intelligence and counterintelligence agency. As such, it now views the PRC as its single largest intelligence and counterintelligence threat. Yet it is clear that the FBI cannot and will not do its job well without the support of affected communities, in particular the Chinese American community. In early 2023, the Committee of 100 pulled together a group of the most senior Chinese Americans who had served in the Justice Department, including former US attorneys and former assistant attorney generals, to meet, off the record, with senior leadership in the Justice Department and the FBI. The message from the group was simple, as former public servants who have dedicated their lives to fighting for American justice and protecting American lives, we sincerely believe that we can enhance our national security while protecting our civil liberties. The two can and must go in lockstep. When we live up to our values and do what America does best, in attracting and retaining the world's best talents, we are impossible to beat.

References

1. Office of the United States Trade Representative (2018) Findings of the investigation into China's acts, policies, and practices related to technology transfer, intellectual property, and innovation under Section 301 of the Trade Act of 1974. Available at: https://ustr.gov/sites/default/files/Section%20301%20FINAL.PDF. Accessed 12 Aug 2025
2. Reuters (2023) Biden orders ban on certain US tech investments in China. Available at: https://www.reuters.com/world/white-house-detail-plans-restricting-some-us-investments-china-source-2023-08-09/. Accessed 12 Aug 2025
3. U.S. Department of Justice (2009) Former Boeing engineer convicted of economic espionage for theft of space shuttle secrets for China. Available at: https://www.justice.gov/opa/pr/former-boeing-engineer-convicted-economic-espionage-theft-space-shuttle-secrets-china. Accessed 12 Aug 2025
4. The New York Times (2023) The daring ruse that exposed China's campaign to steal American secrets. Available at: https://www.nytimes.com/2023/03/07/magazine/china-spying-intellectual-property.html. Accessed 12 Aug 2025
5. U.S. Department of Justice (2022) Chinese government intelligence officer sentenced to 20 years in prison for espionage crimes and attempting to steal trade secrets from aviation and aerospace companies. Available at: https://www.justice.gov/opa/pr/chinese-government-intelligence-officer-sentenced-20-years-prison-espionage-crimes-attempting. Accessed 12 Aug 2025
6. The Wall Street Journal (2023) Nikki Haley: My plan to confront the Chinese threat. Available at: https://www.wsj.com/articles/my-plan-to-confront-the-chinese-threat-tech-transfer-military-farmland-1d5fbda5. Accessed 12 Aug 2025
7. Committee of 100 (2021) Committee of 100 releases findings from research on the economic espionage act. Available at: https://www.committee100.org/wp-content/uploads/2021/09/FINAL-Press-Release-EEA-research-.pdf. Accessed 12 Aug 2025
8. China IPR (2019) The 600 billion dollar China IP echo chamber. Available at: https://chinaipr.com/2019/05/12/the-600-billion-dollar-china-ip-echo-chamber/. Accessed 12 Aug 2025

9. Organisation for Economic Co-operation and Development (2009) Magnitude of counterfeiting and piracy of tangible products: An update. Available at: https://web-archive.oecd.org/2012-06-14/112164-44088872.pdf. Accessed 12 Aug 2025
10. U.S. International Trade Commission (2011) China: Effects of intellectual property infringement and indigenous innovation policies on the U.S. economy. Available at: https://www.usitc.gov/publications/332/pub4226.pdf. Accessed 12 Aug 2025
11. Mercatus Center (2019) How the United States should respond to China's intellectual property practices. Available at: https://www.mercatus.org/research/policy-briefs/how-united-states-should-respond-chinas-intellectual-property-practices. Accessed 12 Aug 2025
12. The National Bureau of Asian Research (n.d.) Commission on the Theft of American Intellectual Property. Available at: https://www.nbr.org/program/commission-on-the-theft-of-intellectual-property/. Accessed 12 Aug 2025
13. MIT Technology Review (2021) The US crackdown on Chinese economic espionage is a mess. We have the data to show it. Available at: https://www.technologyreview.com/2021/12/02/1040656/china-initative-us-justice-department/. Accessed 12 Aug 2025
14. Federal Bureau of Investigation (2020) The threat posed by the Chinese government and the Chinese Communist Party to the economic and national security of the United States. Available at: https://www.fbi.gov/news/speeches/the-threat-posed-by-the-chinese-government-and-the-chinese-communist-party-to-the-economic-and-national-security-of-the-united-states. Accessed 12 Aug 2025
15. The White House (2015) Remarks by President Obama and President Xi of the People's Republic of China in joint press conference. Available at: https://obamawhitehouse.archives.gov/the-press-office/2015/09/25/remarks-president-obama-and-president-xi-peoples-republic-china-joint. Accessed 12 Aug 2025
16. U.S. Department of Justice (2021) Four Chinese nationals working with Ministry of State Security charged with global computer intrusion campaign targeting intellectual property and confidential business information, including infectious disease research. Available at: https://www.justice.gov/opa/pr/four-chinese-nationals-working-ministry-state-security-charged-global-computer-intrusion. Accessed 12 Aug 2025
17. Center for Strategic and International Studies (2018) How much have the Chinese actually taken? Available at: https://www.csis.org/analysis/how-much-have-chinese-actually-taken. Accessed 12 Aug 2025

18. General Motors China (2019) General Motors in China. Available at: https://news.gm.com.cn/en/home/newsroom.detail.html/Pages/news/cn/en/2019/Nov/About-GMChina.html. Accessed 12 Aug 2025
19. Reuters (2023) China car sales return to growth in August, Tesla nearly doubles EV share. Available at: https://www.reuters.com/business/autos-transportation/china-car-sales-return-growth-aug-tesla-nearly-doubles-ev-share-2023-09-08/. Accessed 12 Aug 2025
20. Nature (2018) China's plan to recruit talented researchers. Available at: https://www.nature.com/articles/d41586-018-00538-z.pdf. Accessed 12 Aug 2025
21. Federal Bureau of Investigation (n.d.) The China threat. Available at: https://www.fbi.gov/investigate/counterintelligence/the-china-threat/chinese-talent-plans. Accessed 12 Aug 2025
22. The New York Times (2020) China's lavish funds lured U.S. scientists. What did it get in return? Available at: https://www.nytimes.com/2020/02/06/us/chinas-lavish-funds-lured-us-scientists-what-did-it-get-in-return.html. Accessed 12 Aug 2025
23. U.S. Attorney's Office, Eastern District of Tennessee (2022) PhD chemist sentenced to 168 months for conspiracy to steal traded secrets, economic espionage, theft of trade secrets, and wire fraud. Available at: https://www.justice.gov/usao-edtn/pr/phd-chemist-sentenced-168-months-conspiracy-steal-traded-secrets-economic-espionage. Accessed 12 Aug 2025
24. Stanford University (2011) Brain drain of China. Available at: https://www-cs-faculty.stanford.edu/people/eroberts/cs201/projects/2010-11/BrainDrain/China.html. Accessed 12 Aug 2025
25. Zweig D (2015) America challenges China's national talent programs. Center for Strategic and International Studies. Available at: https://csis-website-prod.s3.amazonaws.com/s3fs-public/publication/20505_zweig_AmericaChallenges_v6_FINAL.pdf. Accessed 12 Aug 2025
26. Crow JM (2022) US–China partnerships bring strength in numbers to big science projects. Nature 603(7900): S6–S8. https://doi.org/10.1038/d41586-022-00570-0
27. Lee, J.J., Haupt, J.P. Winners and losers in US–China scientific research collaborations. High Educ 80, 57–74 (2020). https://doi.org/10.1007/s10734-019-00464-7
28. JASON (2019) Fundamental Research Security: JASON Report. Available at: https://www.nsf.gov/news/special_reports/jasonsecurity/JSR-19-2IFundamentalResearchSecurity_12062019FINAL.pdf. Accessed 12 Aug 2025.
29. National Science Foundation (2024) NSF announcement of the JASON report on fundamental research security. Available at: https://bit.ly/4ajpFvv. Accessed 12 Aug 2025.

30. Business Insider (2018) The director of the FBI says the whole of Chinese society is a threat to the US—and that Americans must step up to defend themselves. Available at: https://www.businessinsider.com/china-threat-to-america-fbi-director-warns-2018-2. Accessed 12 Aug 2025.
31. U.S. House of Representatives (2021) Roundtable led by Reps. Raskin and Chu hears about effects of ethnic profiling against Chinese American scientists. Available at: https://raskin.house.gov/2021/6/roundtable-led-by-reps-raskin-and-chu-hears-about-effects-of-ethnic-profiling-against-chinese-american-scientists. Accessed 12 Aug 2025.
32. Committee of 100 (2021) New Research Shows Significant Racial Disparities Against Chinese and Asians in Espionage Prosecutions. Available at: https://www.committee100.org/wp-content/uploads/2021/09/FINAL-Press-Release-EEA-research-.pdf. Accessed 12 Aug 2025.
33. U.S. Senate Committee on Commerce, Science, and Transportation (2021) Committee Investigation Report: Abuse and misconduct at the Commerce Department. Available at: https://www.commerce.senate.gov/services/files/3893917C-A6CE-4D6C-AA9D-781401322BF3. Accessed 12 Aug 2025.
34. NBC News (2023) After being wrongfully accused of spying for China, professor wins appeal to sue the government. Available at: https://www.nbcnews.com/news/asian-america/wrongfully-accused-spying-china-professor-wins-appeal-sue-government-rcna86109. Accessed 12 Aug 2025.
35. NBC News (2022) MIT professor wrongfully accused of spying for China helps make major discovery. Available at: https://www.nbcnews.com/news/asian-america/mit-professor-wrongfully-accused-spying-china-helps-make-major-discove-rcna44637. Accessed 12 Aug 2025.
36. MIT Faculty Newsletter (2021) Faculty letter to President Reif in support of Professor Gang Chen. Available at: https://fnl.mit.edu/january-february-2021/faculty-letter-to-president-reif-in-support-of-professor-gang-chen/. Accessed 12 Aug 2025.
37. Winds of Freedom (2021) Letter from Stanford University Faculty to Garland. Available at: https://sites.google.com/view/winds-of-freedom. Accessed 12 Aug 2025.
38. Science (2023) Pall of suspicion. Available at: https://www.science.org/content/article/pall-suspicion-nihs-secretive-china-initiative-destroyed-scores-academic-careers. Accessed 12 Aug 2025.
39. South China Morning Post (2024) China-born neuroscientist Jane Wu lost her US lab. Then she lost her life. Available at: https://www.scmp.com/news/china/science/article/3276370/china-born-neuroscientist-jane-wu-lost-her-us-lab-then-she-lost-her-life. Accessed 12 Aug 2025.

40. Committee of 100 (2021) Racial Profiling Among Scientists of Chinese Descent and Consequences for the U.S. Scientific Community. Available at: https://www.committee100.org/wp-content/uploads/2021/10/C100-Lee-Li-White-Paper-FINAL-FINAL-10.28.pdf. Accessed 12 Aug 2025.
41. Yu Xie, Ju Li, Qian He et al. (2023) Caught in the crossfire: Fears of Chinese American scientists. PNAS 120(12): e2216248120. https://doi.org/10.1073/pnas.2216248120
42. Princeton University (2023) Caught in the crossfire: fears of Chinese American scientists. Available at: https://collaborate.princeton.edu/en/publications/caught-in-the-crossfire-fears-of-chinese-american-scientists. Accessed 12 Aug 2025.
43. Wall Street Journal (2022) U.S.–China tensions fuel outflow of Chinese scientists from U.S. universities. Available at: https://www.wsj.com/articles/u-s-china-tensions-fuel-outflow-of-chinese-scientists-from-u-s-universities-11663866938. Accessed 12 Aug 2025.
44. Committee of 100 (n.d.) Thematic report on Chinese American contributions: Entrepreneurship and Business Leadership. Available at: Available at: https://www.committee100.org/our-work/from-foundations-to-frontiers/. Accessed 12 Aug 2025.
45. Fierce Network (2018) Huawei equipment currently deployed by 25 U.S. rural wireless carriers, RWA says. Available at: https://www.fiercewireless.com/wireless/huawei-equipment-currently-deployed-by-25-u-s-rural-wireless-carriers-rwa-says. Accessed 12 Aug 2025.
46. Wall Street Journal (2024) Huawei's return is case study in U.S. power and its limits. Available at: https://www.wsj.com/business/telecom/huaweis-return-is-case-study-in-u-s-powerand-its-limits-b6175cff. Accessed 12 Aug 2025.
47. New York Times (2022) For China's Auto Market, Electric Isn't the Future. It's the Present. Available at: https://www.nytimes.com/2022/09/26/business/china-electric-vehicles.html. Accessed 12 Aug 2025.
48. Wall Street Journal (2024) How China is churning out EVs faster than everyone else. Available at: https://www.wsj.com/business/autos/how-china-is-churning-out-evs-faster-than-everyone-else-df316c71. Accessed 12 Aug 2025.
49. Electrek (2025) China breaks records as global EV sales hit 7.2 million in 2025. Available at: https://electrek.co/2025/06/12/china-breaks-records-as-global-ev-sales-hit-7-2-million-in-2025. Accessed 12 Aug 2025.
50. New York Times (2025) How Republican E.V. Cuts Could Put U.S. Carmakers Behind China. Available at: https://www.nytimes.com/2025/07/02/business/ev-cars-us-china-trump.html. Accessed 12 Aug 2025.

51. University of Northern Iowa (1987) The U.S. Automakers' Reaction to the Japanese. Available at: https://scholarworks.uni.edu/cgi/viewcontent.cgi?article=1030&context=draftings. Accessed 12 Aug 2025.
52. National Science Board, National Science Foundation (2020) Science and engineering indicators 2020: The state of U.S. science & engineering. Report No. NSB-2020–1. Alexandria, VA. Available at: https://ncses.nsf.gov/pubs/nsb20201/u-s-and-global-education. Accessed 12 Aug 2025.
53. U.S. House Select Committee on the CCP (2025) Chairman Moolenaar Demands Transparency from Universities on National Security Risks Posed by Chinese Nationals in STEM Programs. Available at: https://selectcommitteeontheccp.house.gov/media/press-releases/chairman-moolenaar-demands-transparency-universities-national-security-risks. Accessed 12 Aug 2025.
54. U.S. Department of State (2025) New visa policies put America first, not China. Available at: https://www.state.gov/releases/office-of-the-spokesperson/2025/05/new-visa-policies-put-america-first-not-china. Accessed 12 Aug 2025.
55. Trump DJ (2025) Truth Social post. Available at: https://truthsocial.com/@realDonaldTrump/posts/114664632971715644. Accessed 12 Aug 2025.
56. Institute of International Education (2024) Open Doors: Student mobility fact sheets. Available at: https://opendoorsdata.org/fact_sheets/student-mobility. Accessed 12 Aug 2025.
57. National Science and Technology Council (2022) NSPM-33 implementation guidance. Available at: https://bidenwhitehouse.archives.gov/wp-content/uploads/2022/01/010422-NSPM-33-Implementation-Guidance.pdf. Accessed 12 Aug 2025.
58. Scientific American (2020) The China threat and the future of global science. Available at: https://blogs.scientificamerican.com/observations/the-china-threat-and-the-future-of-global-science. Accessed 12 Aug 2025.
59. MIT (2022) University engagement with China: An MIT approach. Available at: https://global.mit.edu/wp-content/uploads/2022/11/FINALUniversity-Engagement-with-China_An-MIT-Approach-Nov2022.pdf. Accessed 12 Aug 2025.
60. China Daily (2023) Xi's remarks on importance of overseas Chinese. Available at: https://www.chinadaily.com.cn/a/202308/31/WS64f09da3a310d2dce4bb3372.html. Accessed 12 Aug 2025.
61. Federal Bureau of Investigation (2022) Diversity statistics report. Formerly available at: https://fbijobs.gov/sites/default/files/2022-05/Report_Diversity.pdf. Accessed 12 Aug 2025.

62. Government Executive (2020) FBI has failed to move the needle on diversity over the past decade despite efforts of recent directors. Available at: https://www.govexec.com/workforce/2020/02/fbi-has-failed-move-needle-diversity-over-past-decade-despite-efforts-recent-directors/163127/. Accessed 12 Aug 2025.

CHAPTER 5

Trade/Economics: The $1.2 Trillion Relationship

Assumption 1: China is the Cause of American Job Loss
Assumption 2: China Will Soon Supplant the US
Assumption 3: China is Laying Debt Traps Around the World

Despite tariffs and sanctions and talks of de-coupling, trade and trade deficit between US and China grew in 2022 [1]. While much focus has been on the trade deficit, it is only part and parcel of the larger economic relationship. According to the Bureau of Economic Analysis at the Commerce Department, in 2022, the US exported $198 billion to China, and imported $564 billion from China. In addition, in 2021, Chinese subsidiaries of US majority owned businesses made $471 billion in China, while US subsidiaries of Chinese firms made $65 billion in the US [2]. Adding the numbers up, and we have a $1.2 trillion economic relationship, with each side roughly equal to the other. Almost all experts I've spoken to agree that this economic relationship forms the linchpin of the bilateral relationship and why it is fundamentally different from the relationship between the US and Soviet Union, which involved very little trade and commerce with each other. While catchy in headlines, the trade deficit with China largely disappears when factored in profits made by American subsidiaries based in China. Due to US tax policies, that profit is largely parked outside the US, which the Tax Cuts and Jobs Act (TCJA) of 2017 attempted to fix [3].

Z. Z. Huang, *Rethinking China*,
https://doi.org/10.1007/978-981-95-3608-5_5

President Trump spoke often of the four million American jobs, primarily in manufacturing, lost to China [4]. On March 15, 2017, Trump said, "our nation has lost over 60,000 factories since China joined the World Trade Organization (WTO)—60,000." Census figures show that 59,794 manufacturing establishments had closed in the US from 2001 through 2015, erasing 4.3 million jobs. But how many were due to China? It has become accepted wisdom in Washington D.C. that China is the primary, if not the exclusive cause of American manufacturing job losses. The "China Shock" refers to the decades after China's ascension into the World Trade Organization in 2001, after which cheap Chinese imports significantly undercut American manufacturing and led to the loss of American jobs, especially in the South Atlantic and Deep South regions. The China Shock was methodically studied in 2013 by MIT economist David Autor and his colleagues David Dorn and Gordon Hanson [5]. In 2021, the three authors followed up with a study on the "Persistence of the China Shock" that showed the hardest hit regions have yet to recover from the rapid declines that they had experienced [6]. Autor, Dorn, and Hanson's research found that China accounted for around 1 million American manufacturing jobs lost between 1999 and 2011, and 2.4 million jobs overall [7]. News stories abound of small towns in America that had lost their manufacturing plants, leading to widespread unemployment and decades of despair and stagnation for the affected communities. Political pundits posit that this was one of the key reasons that traditional manufacturing regions turned away from Democrats and voted for Donald Trump in 2016.

I connected with two of the three authors, David Autor, Professor of Economics at MIT, and Gordon Hanson, Professor in Urban Policy at Harvard Kennedy School. I was expecting David and Gordon to educate me on the scale and magnitude of damages inflicted on American workers by China's rise. Indeed, both authors spoke eloquently about the loss of American manufacturing jobs after China's admission into the WTO, especially in geographical areas where Americans are less mobile, less educated, and with fewer diversified industries. Both spoke about the furniture or shoe manufacturer that left the US, never to return [6]. And both spoke about the persistence of the China Shock on the most affected communities, even though much of the job losses occurred before 2011. Yet the conversations quickly turned in ways that I did not anticipate.

Gordon brought up US job gains due to trade with China. With cheaper Chinese components and manufactured goods, innovative American firms, in particular on the coasts, created higher paid jobs for higher educated and more mobile Americans. Gordon offered Apple as an example. Apple significantly increased its profit margin and hired more designers, engineers, and marketers thanks to its ability to source lower cost and high quality manufacturing goods and components from China. Gordon believed that without China, job losses in small towns would still have occurred but perhaps more incrementally. Inevitably, globalization would reach and affect regions with less educated and less mobile workers more disproportionately. The real question political leaders should be asking is how local economies better manage the concentrated downsides of globalization. When I spoke with David, he echoed Gordon's assertion that China's ascension to the WTO helped the American middle class but hurt America's manufacturing base. He further noted that the battle over traditional manufacturing is a battle that has been fought and lost. The focus now must be on how best to manage the new energy transition that will involve high-end manufacturing, and how better to help people still trapped in regions without the influx of new jobs.

The estimate by both authors is that on average, it's a wash between jobs lost and jobs gained due to trade with China. I asked them if there is data to support this claim, and they directed me to Nicolas Bloom, Professor of Economics at Stanford. In 2019, Nicolas and colleagues published a paper titled "The Impact of Chinese Trade on US Employment: the Good, the Bad, and the Debatable [8]." The paper concluded that the China Shock between 1990 and 2014 did not cause net negative effects on aggregate US employment. The China shock instead catalyzed a geographic reallocation of American economic activities away from areas with lower levels of education to areas with higher levels of education. Varying geographical effects of the China Shock may have contributed to growing regional inequality and political polarization in the US [9]. When I spoke with Nicolas, he was quick to point out that as an Englishman living in America, his research interests extended beyond the effects of China's rise in the US to its effects in Europe as well. In 2016, he and colleagues published a paper titled "Trade Induced Technical Change? The Impact of Chinese Imports on Innovation, IT and Productivity [10]." Examining performance and total firm productivity of more than half a million firms in 12 European countries from 1996 to 2007, he found that import competition from China accounted for 14% of European technological upgrading between 2000 to 2007. He believes that gains to innovation and productivity are underappreciated in the current debate on China, but may ultimately outweigh the costs of trade competition with China [11]. While no comparable research has been conducted in the US, he surmises that it's realistic to imagine similar effects of China's rise to innovation and productivity in the US. In 2018, Zhi Wang, Research Professor in the Schar School of Policy and Government at George Mason University, along with colleagues, published a study that calculated a broader supply chain effect of the China Shock, including how cheaper intermediate inputs from China—such as laptops, printers, and office machine parts—have led to cost savings for US firms, improving their efficiency and adding to US jobs. The study concluded that trading with China yielded a positive boost overall to American employment and real wages [12].

Nicolas reaffirmed David and Gordon's argument that the China Shock is largely a phenomenon from twenty years ago. As the horse has bolted from the gates, there is no turning back. Today, he sees the American service sector going global in front of our eyes, and this time American service jobs are going to India, the Philippines, and a whole host of new competitor countries. The urgency should be to multiply what successful American firms such as Levi Strauss has achieved domestically. Even as Levi Strauss closed down its American factories in the early 2000s, today it has more employees in San Francisco because of continued innovation and upgrading. America can and must continuously move up the value chain, just as it did in response to the China Shock.

The assumption that China is the cause of American job losses is misleading and counterproductive because it focuses on the jobs of yesterday, without due consideration for the positive effects of China's rise to the entire American value chain. Preliminary evidence suggests that retaliatory measures based on this assumption have hurt rather than helped Americans most affected by the China Shock. Pablo Fajgelbaum, Professor of Economics at UCLA and colleagues found that Trump's trade war impacted his Republican base most negatively, as retaliatory tariffs targeted heavily Republican counties. Broadly, Trump's tariffs on China have been passed onto American consumers almost dollar for dollar [13]. China's dominance in key strategic industries such as rare earth elements—needed to make weapons, electronics, and a range of consumer goods—also makes tariffs and retaliatory trade measures that much more costly [14]. Instead, our focus should be on the jobs of tomorrow, and to strengthen our preparedness to deal with the uneven benefits and concentrated hurts of globalization. As the two authors of the China Shock repeatedly stressed to me, the lesson of the China Shock isn't that trade is bad for America—it's that the concentrated and long-lasting impacts of job loss require our attention [15].

In recent years, the prevalent assumption has been that China will soon overtake the US as the world's largest economy. This assumption paired with the previous assumption that China's economic growth comes at the expense of American jobs, fuels the fear of American economic decline and demise. In 2023, the nominal US GDP stands at $26.85 trillion, while the Chinese GDP stands at $19.37 trillion [16]. China is 72% of the US economy. The comparison becomes even less impressive when taking into account that China has a population of 1.425 billion and the US a population of 340 million. The per capita GDP in the US is 5.78 times higher than that in China. Put it another way, an American produces 5.78 times the goods and services of a Chinese, on average. Even after accounting for purchasing power parity, the per capita GDP in the US is 3.61 times higher than that in China. With Chinese GDP growth slowing down significantly, it is not clear when China will overtake the US [17].

A useful frame of reference that has been brought to my attention is to see the US and China as having very comparable economic problems. Both countries struggle with income inequality, an aging population, unaffordable housing prices, lack of job opportunities, especially for youth, and rising healthcare costs, in particular for retirees and the elderly. Both countries deal with governments that take on too much debt and make as many bad economic decisions as good ones. Speak to any Chinese and he'll attest to the fact that the engine of economic growth in China is the private entrepreneur. Private enterprises contribute approximately 60% of China's GDP, 70% of its innovative capacity, 80% of urban employment, and 90% of new jobs [18]. Having started a business in China I can attest to the drive, ingenuity, and hunger of the typical Chinese entrepreneur. As a billionaire Chinese entrepreneur remarked to me, "Mr. Huang, you know the Chinese entrepreneur. Give him a little daylight and he'll find a way to succeed." Today, the PRC government has prioritized State Owned Enterprises (SOEs) over private firms, and national security over economic growth. China's economy overtaking that of the US is not inevitable.

Yet when it comes to debating the Chinese economy, even vaulted authorities tend to toggle between extremes. In growing the financial services data company, I had pitched to and brought onboard as clients hundreds of investment firms on Wall Street, including multi-billion dollar hedge funds and mutual funds. Even among some of the best investment minds on Wall Street, the common refrain is either "China will rule the world," or "China is a house of cards about to fall." Very rarely do I hear a nuanced analysis of the strengths and weaknesses of the Chinese economy. Yes, China has been in a housing crisis since 2020, with many real-estate developers awash in unfinished projects and unpayable debt. In December 2021, Evergrande, one of the largest developers in China, defaulted on $300 billion in liabilities [19]. Yet this was brought on in large measures by the PRC government, in its efforts to curb excessive borrowing and speculation in the housing market. Post-pandemic, consumer spending and sentiments are significantly down in China, leading to extensive youth unemployment and economic uncertainty. Yet unlike the United States, which unleashed close to $5 trillion dollars of COVID-19 stimulus (CARES Act $2.2 trillion, Paycheck Protection Program and Health-care Enhancement Act $484 billion, Consolidated Appropriations Act $900 billion, American Rescue Plan $1.9 trillion), the PRC government's COVID-19 stimulus (approximately $500–800 billion) was minuscule in comparison. Therefore, while US inflation rates increased from 1.4% in 2020 to 7% in 2021 and 8% in 2022, China's inflation rate remained steady between 1 and 2% post pandemic. The US economy contracted by 3.4% in 2020 due to COVID-19, and grew by 5.9% in 2021, 2.1% in 2022 and 1.9% in 2023. The Chinese economy grew by 2.3% in 2023 despite COVID-19, and 8.4% in 2021, 3% in 2022 and 5% in 2023. These numbers are substantially down from historical trends but not close to suggesting a crumbling of the economic house. Just as we in America are still grappling with the positives and negatives of our own government's economic policymaking, we should reserve our judgment and monitor closely the positives and negatives of China's approaches.

Beyond measuring the US–China economic relationship in quantitative terms—in per capita GDP or GDP growth—we should also measure it qualitatively, in particular in developments in advanced technologies. The technology de-coupling initiated under President Trump continued and intensified under the Biden administration. How will it affect China? In 2022, Wei Jiang, Vice Dean for Faculty and Research and Professor of Finance at Emory University, along with colleagues, published a paper mapping US–China technology de-coupling and dependence [20]. The authors placed particular focus on patents in 10 high tech fields: smartphones, semiconductors, software, pharmaceuticals, internal combustion engines, machine learning, neural networks, drones, cloud computing, and self-driving cars. Among the 10 high tech fields analyzed, China's dependence on the US is the greatest in pharmaceuticals, semiconductors, software, and smartphones, but their dependence levels had decreased over time. Most of the more decoupled fields are relatively new technologies, such as neural networks, cloud computing, and self-driving cars [21]. The jury may still be out on whether technology de-coupling with China will in the long run benefit American businesses by handicapping their Chinese competition, or hurt American businesses by shutting them off from the lucrative Chinese market and fostering local competition.

Yet at least in the critically important field of artificial intelligence, the latter seems to be true. Despite export controls on AI chipset and fabrication equipment sold to China and sanctions on an ever-growing list of Chinese firms, with the release of its R1 model on January 20, 2025—the same day as President Trump's second inauguration—Chinese firm DeepSeek has cemented its reputation as a top-tier AI research firm globally. Notable is that DeepSeek's technical team appears to have been educated and trained almost entirely in China, rather than at Western universities or Western companies. Taken broadly, the gap between the US and China in AI has "narrowed significantly, and it is unrealistic to expect a lead of more than a year or two, even with extremely aggressive export controls," noted a report by CSIS [22]. In an interview with Stratechery, Nvidia CEO Jensen Huang said the bans—including the prohibition of Nvidia's H20 AI chip tailored for China—are backfiring. Rather than weakening China's AI capabilities, the restrictions drive Chinese firms like Huawei to develop their own AI chips, reducing reliance on US technology and shrinking Nvidia's once dominant market share in the country. Huang highlighted that Nvidia controlled 95% of the Chinese market in early 2021, but its share has since fallen to about 50% due to the impact of both Trump and Biden era sanctions. Despite these measures, China's AI industry is not slowing down. Companies like Tencent and Alibaba now purchase locally developed AI chips, fueling domestic research, development, and innovation. Huang also warned of the economic costs tied to these policies. Nvidia had to write off $5.5 billion in potential sales and walk away from $15 billion worth of business. He estimated a loss of $3 billion in tax revenue for the US and losing out on a Chinese AI market worth $50 billion annually. He concluded that leaving such a large ecosystem behind poses the biggest long-term threat to Nvidia's proprietary AI platform [23]. While the US government still believes that it retains a full range of options, its options are more limited now, with our escalations met with Chinese escalations, and the difficulty of the Chinese trusting us fully even if we decided to do away with the controls.

In one area, however, the roles of the US and China have reversed, and that deserves special attention: the US is now the world's largest debtor nation, and China the world's largest creditor nation. After World War II, when most of the world laid in ruins, the US became the world's greatest creditor nation, holding 70% of the world's gold reserve. The Marshall Plan, announced by Secretary of State George Marshall in 1947, provided US funding to sixteen European countries. A total of $13.6 billion (equivalent to $165 billion in 2025 money) was appropriated for the plan. By 1950, the participating countries had returned to, or exceeded, their prewar production levels [24]. In 2013, President Xi announced the Belt and Road Initiative (BRI), arguably the most ambitious global trade and infrastructure program in modern history [25]. BRI launched on a confluence of favorable conditions: China's burgeoning foreign reserve, Chinese expertise in infrastructure building from four decades of domestic expansion, excessive Chinese export capacity, and a desire to link new markets. To date, China has invested over $1 trillion in over 10,000 projects across 165 countries.

I first heard about the BRI when I was an entrepreneur in China, and later learned more about it when I served as Special Assistant to the USAID administrator. My role at USAID permitted me to join a series of White House led strategic planning discussions on reevaluating America's approach to international aid. The series was led by then Special Assistant to the President, and later USAID administrator, Samantha Power. While American and Western aid had focused primarily on capacity building, technical training, and disease eradication, China focused on building roads, railways, power plants, ports, and other infrastructure projects. My curiosity was doubly piqued because I was hearing positive feedback on the BRI from development experts within USAID but ominous warnings from senior political appointees. For most of the last decade, the focus by American politicians and the media has been on what hasn't worked well with the BRI, including unfinished projects, official corruption, local labor disputes, environmental degradation, poor construction quality, predatory lending, and debt traps leading to asset seizures and takeovers.

I spoke to Deborah Brautigam, Professor and Director of the China Africa Research Initiative, at Johns Hopkins' School of Advanced International Studies. Deborah has dedicated her life to tracking China's development efforts in Africa. She quickly pointed out and dispelled three myths around China's development work in Africa. First. white elephant or unfinished projects—her data suggested a few but not many. Second, exclusive use of Chinese workers—reality on the ground is close to 80% local versus 20% Chinese workers simply because it's too expensive to bring Chinese workers to Africa. XThird, debt trap diplomacy—not factual because China doesn't need debt leverage to buy into ports and mines.

In a 2021 article in the Atlantic titled "The Chinese Debt Trap is a Myth," Deborah cited the example of the Sri Lankan port of Hambantota, which has been quoted at length by US government officials [26]. As the story goes, Beijing pushed Sri Lanka into borrowing money from Chinese banks to pay for the project, which had no prospect of commercial success. Onerous terms and feeble revenues eventually pushed Sri Lanka into default, at which point Beijing demanded the port as collateral, forcing the Sri Lankan government to surrender control to a Chinese firm. The whole episode was a Chinese design to militarize the port. Deborah wrote that the truth is stubbornly different. Armed with Canadian and Dutch reports of project feasibility, the Sri Lankan government had earlier approached the US and India on Hambantota; both countries declined. A Chinese construction firm, China Harbor Group, learned about Colombo's aspirations, lobbied hard for and received the project. China Eximbank offered a $307 million, 15-year commercial loan with a 4-year grace period, offering Sri Lanka a choice between a 6.3% fixed interest rate or one that would rise or fall depending on LIBOR, a floating rate. When a new Sri Lankan government took office in 2015, Sri Lanka owed more to Japan, the World Bank, and the Asian Development Bank than to China. Of the $4.5 billion in debt service Sri Lanka would pay in 2017, only 5% was because of Hambantota. The new government decided to raise much-needed dollars by leasing out the underperforming Hambantota Port to China Merchants, making it the majority shareholder with a 99-year lease, and used the $1.12 billion cash infusion to bolster its foreign reserves, not to pay off China. As to the concern that Hambantota could become a "forward military base" for China, the port is cut into the coast to avoid the Indian Ocean's heavy swells, and its narrow channel allows only one ship to enter or exit at a time, typically with the aid of a tugboat. In the event of a military conflict, naval vessels stationed there would be proverbial fish in a barrel. Further research by Deborah confirmed that Chinese banks willingly restructure the terms of existing loans and have never actually seized an asset from any country, much less the port of Hambantota.

The AID Data Lab at the College of William and Mary hosts arguably the largest data repository on Chinese investments overseas. The lab has been meticulously tracking loans and grants from official sector institutions in China in 20,985 projects across 165 low- and middle-income countries worth $1.34 trillion. Its China Global Development Finance Dataset 3.0, released in November 2023, tracks projects over 22 commitment years (2000–2021) and provides details on the timing of project implementation over a 24-year period (2000–2023) [27]. The lab has also obtained more than 100 unredacted loan documents between China and recipient countries and is in the process of sorting through 200 more. I had an opportunity to speak with multiple members of the AID Data Lab team. Primarily, I wanted to know how many projects were actually completed, as incomplete projects signal likely failure, and possible debt troubles for recipient countries. The data showed that between 2000 and 2017, more than 3800 infrastructure projects were committed, with 2900 of these projects having been completed, reflecting a completion rate of over 75%. The data also showed that China has not been interested in taking over illiquid assets.

When it comes to assessing the impact of completed projects, I was told of the 759 km long Addis Ababa–Djibouti Railway ("Yali Railway"), the only railway line connecting landlocked Ethiopia with a Djibouti Port. The railway begins at Sebeta, just outside of Ethiopia's capital of Addis Ababa. The line then runs southeast to Modjo and Adama, both towns located in the Ethiopian Great Rift Valley. At Modjo, the railway connects to the Modjo Dry Port, Ethiopia's most important inland dry port as well as its main hub for domestic and international freight services. At Adama, the railway turns northeast towards Dire Dawa. Crossing the Ethiopia-Djibouti border between Dewale and Ali Sabieh, the line reaches the Djibouti passenger terminal at Nagad railway station, near Djibouti–Ambouli International Airport. The completion of the Addis Ababa–Djibouti Railway has turned a travel time of over seven days into a 10-hour affair. Since commencing operations in June 2022, the rail has facilitated 463,096 trips and 6.46 million tons of goods, with transportation income expanding 35% annually. The railway has become a key part of Ethiopia's trade network, reportedly carrying around 90% of its exports. What really surprised me was what Sheng Zhang, Research Analyst at AID Data Lab, shared with me. While much Western media attention has been focused on Chinese investments in energy and transportation, between 2000 and 2021, health and education stood as major areas of Chinese overseas investments, with the health sector recording more than 3700 project, and the education sector covering over 2600 projects [28].

The ancient Silk Road connected China with Europe through Central Asia and the Middle East for more than a thousand years. In fact, Christopher Columbus, and before him, the Portuguese explorers, embarked on their perilous ocean expeditions because they wanted to find alternative routes to the Silk Road, after key passages fell under the dominion of the Ottoman empire. In no small way, the age of exploration and European colonialism arose because of the importance of the Silk Road and the trade between the West and East. Fast forward to today, China is not laying debt traps around the world because it is more benevolent or altruistic. It is laying infrastructure and connecting trade routes around the world because it believes in the long-term economic benefits. China has become the top trading partner of over 120 countries, and finished infrastructure projects such as roads, railways, power plants, ports, etc. throw off positive externalities, including increased economic growth, trade, and commerce [29]. If only 75% of BRI succeeds, and there's every indication that the Chinese will adjust and modify but continue the initiative, we will still see immense increases in trade and commerce, and future service and technology offerings to boot. The assumption that China is laying debt traps around the world is false and detrimental to our national interest because it blinds us from seeing the forest for the trees. While individual BRI projects may be problematic and some loans are issued at high rates, the US cannot and must not discount the opportunities that arise from sustained investments in infrastructure and trade routes in the developing world. With the US on the sidelines, it risks losing the Global South.

Better assumptions can be:

Assumption 1: The US Should Invest in the Jobs of the Future
Assumption 2: The US Must be Strategic in its Industrial Policy

Assumption 3: The US Can Succeed in the Global South without Copying China

Our world is changing rapidly not just because of globalization but even more so with the unprecedented advancements in technology. Similar to globalization, technological change impacts areas with lower educated, less mobile workers more disproportionately. Both Autor and Hanson provided insights on how the US could invest in the jobs of the future and combat a legacy of joblessness and social dislocation in hard hit regions. They believed that we should (1) help non college educated workers with community college certification and training, (2) dedicate programs to assist small- and medium-size businesses, and (3) attract new firms and talents to underrepresented regions. COVID-19 has shown that remote workers can live anywhere, and many hitherto overlooked regions offer lower cost of living, access to the outdoors, easier commute and a more relaxed pace of life. Columbus, Ohio is often cited as an example, with firms such as Wells Fargo, Intel, Google, and Honda moving there and setting up shops. Gordon pointed me to the Reimaging the Economy Project at the Harvard Kennedy School, set up in 2022 to explore how we might build an economy at once productive and inclusive [30]. Notably, he mentioned that most countries have an active worker policy to help manage the effects of globalization, citing Denmark as an example in its efforts to mitigate the loss of traditional textile jobs. Interestingly, Autor and Hanson explicitly included encouraging Chinese manufacturing in the US as a key element for revitalizing US industry and reducing overreliance on foreign supply chains [31].

Ro Khanna represents California's 17th Congressional District, located in the heart of Silicon Valley. He is also the author of "Dignity in a Digital Age, Making Tech Work for all of us," and "Entrepreneurial Nation, Why Manufacturing is Still Key to America's Future." I sat down with him over coffee in Washington D.C. and later spoke with him over the phone. Ro believes that with effective government and private sector partnerships, it is possible to build advanced manufacturing capabilities all across the US. The US government can make loans, invest in new technologies and worker training programs, and entice American firms to re-invest in America. With an annual IT budget of $80 billion, US government contracts can target underrepresented communities and geographies. He referenced Google's program with historically black colleges and universities that trains Black students in digital careers [32].

Fundamental to his belief is that the manufacturing jobs of tomorrow are technology jobs, because technology enables factories to be more efficient and cost-effective.

In my conversations with congressional offices across the political aisle, all underscored the fact that due to the perceived economic threat from China, legislations that have not moved in a long time have been implemented, including the Bipartisan Infrastructure Law, the CHIPS and Science Act, and the Inflation Reduction Act. The joke is that the Inflation Reduction Act has inflation reduction in title only, the rest is about increased funding to compete with China on renewable energy and electric vehicles. The hope is that the three bills, totaling over $2 trillion, would spur creation in the jobs of the future, in clean energy, semiconductor manufacturing, and electric vehicle adoption. While it is politically expedient to use a foreign rival to spur domestic investments, we must be mindful of the checkered history of industrial policy.

Industrial policy is defined as a set of government policies that support specific industries or economic activities. Industrial policy has largely fallen out of favor in the US based on the belief that the market and not the government should determine winners and losers [33]. The rise of China has made industrial policy suddenly fashionable again, yet very little public discourse has been had on how best to spend the $2 trillion in American industrial policy funding. In 2022, the Stanford Center on China's Economy and Institutions and the Asia Society Policy Institute's Center for China Analysis co-organized a closed-door roundtable on the scope, impact, and implications of China's industrial policy. China—compared to seven other major economies including Germany, the US, Japan, South Korea, France, Taiwan, and Brazil—is an outlier in terms of the scope and scale of its industrial policy spending. Its total spending, conservatively calculated, amounted to at least 1.7% of China's GDP in 2019, or over $248 billion. China spends far more than any other economy, whether measured as a percentage of its GDP or in dollar amounts. When using a more flexible definition of industrial spending—such as government procurement of goods from domestic firms—it is estimated that China's industrial policy spending totals 5% of the country's GDP [34, 35].

Yet China's industrial policy is notable for its outcome variations. In the wind industry, for example, Beijing's protectionist policies sought to restrict multinational firms with localization, technology transfer, and joint venture requirements. Beijing also actively tried to push its wind industry by leapfrogging technologies to gain first-mover advantages. The industry scored some technological successes, but the sector failed to develop in other, equally valuable ways, such as in design, supply chain adaptability, dynamism, and depth of capacity. By contrast, the government chose not to intervene in the country's solar industry. Yet, the solar industry scored remarkable successes through incremental innovation. Solar firms localized the entire supply chain, scaled up, and lowered costs. Because domestic demand did not exist at the time, they exported their solar products overseas. To succeed, China's solar firms had to meet stringent quality standards appropriate for international markets. Impressively, China's solar firms successfully penetrated global markets. They also achieved first-generation technological breakthroughs. These two comparative cases are illustrative of two points. First, there are both successes and failures in China's state-led support for new technologies. Second, industrial policy is distortionary, resulting in inefficient allocation of capital and resources. State-led support may even be the "kiss of death" for some sectors [36].

Under President Hu Jintao, President Xi's predecessor, the PRC government unveiled the Medium- and Long-Term Science and Technology Plan (2006–2020) that focused on indigenous innovation in sixteen key target sectors, among which is next-generation broadband wireless mobile technologies [37]. The idea is to catch up through indigenous innovation, using China's immense market to develop intellectual property solely for China, in the hope of cornering the domestic market and setting up competitive local firms that can eventually go global. In China, the largest and most expensive experiment on state sponsored innovation took place—a $50 billion dollar re-shaping of the domestic telecommunications industry—in which I had a front row seat.

The PRC government developed its own 3G standard, TD-SCDMA (Time Division Synchronous Code Division Multiple Access), as an alternative to international 3G standards. The technology was recognized in 1999 by the International Telecommunication Union (ITU), a United Nations—affiliated body that coordinates global wireless technologies and spectrum use. But paper recognition meant little when the technology had scant market support and was viewed as pedestrian and relevant only within China. By the end of 2006—after seven consecutive years of delaying 3G licensing—the PRC government could no longer avoid a decision on TD-SCDMA. It recognized that China could not advance the standard on its own and required foreign partners. In my role as co-Managing Director of Intel China's WiMax Program Office, alongside my colleague Rong Peng, I was in charge of Intel's telecommunications efforts in China and led our engagement strategy. In 2006, Intel signed a Memorandum of Understanding with the Ministry of Information and Industry on next-generation wireless technology collaboration and co-development. Chinese firms were quick to jump on the government's bandwagon. Yet after more than $50 billion spent, $34 billion by China Mobile alone, the experiment was unceremoniously shut down in 2014 [38]. The lesson learned seems obvious in hindsight: while generous government funding can prop up a technology for a short time, if the product is inferior or there is no clear market advantage, no amount of government money can sustain an industrial policy. The US must be thoughtful and strategic in our industrial policies, and not try to out-China.

The $280 billion CHIPS and Science Act, signed into law in late 2022, proposes to bring semiconductor manufacturing back to America [39]. Within the $280 billion, $52.7 billion is slated for semiconductor manufacturing, R&D, and workforce development, with Intel expected to be the largest beneficiary. I spoke with the author of "Chip War," Chris Miller, who is an Assistant Professor of International History at the Fletcher School of Law and Diplomacy at Tufts University. His book chronicles the decades-long battle to control what has emerged as the world's most critical resource—microchip technology—with the US and China increasingly in conflict. Adding to the tension is that the most advanced semiconductor manufacturing facilities in the world, run by TSMC, are based in Taiwan. Chris believes that the CHIPS Act is a step in the right direction. I asked him to explain how the CHIPS Act may bend the curve on market forces that have largely driven semiconductor manufacturing out of the US. With Intel and Micron as notable exceptions, most American firms have outsourced their semiconductor manufacturing because it takes $1–10 billion every 2–3 years to build out a new semiconductor fab. It simply makes no business sense to do it yourself when someone else, in Taiwan or South Korea or China, can do it cheaper and better. While $52.7 billion may sound like a large number, in effect it may only be sufficient for a few fabs for one cycle. Already we are seeing TSMC fab delays in Arizona [40] and Intel fab delays in Ohio due to cost overruns and shortage of qualified staff [41]. Chris pointed out that *if* the initial fabs proved to be successful, the CHIPS Act includes investment tax credits that may be extended in the future.

To learn more, I spoke with Aaron (Ronnie) Chatterji, Professor of Business and Public Policy at Duke University, who just returned from serving as the White House CHIPS Act Coordinator and Acting Deputy Director of the National Economic Council. Ronnie concurred that industrial policy has not been studied with sufficient depth in recent years by American academics or bureaucrats, but argued that we must try because America could lose our competitive edge in innovation if we outsource manufacturing capabilities overseas, whether in semiconductor or in renewable energy. He conceded that there is a steep curve on cost and capability that American firms must catch up to against entrenched Asian competitors. His hope is that the margin of difference can be somewhat compensated by buyers willing to pay for supply chain resilience. I asked him what long-term incentives Asian firms, such as TSMC, have to base their most advanced semiconductor fabs in the US when the costs are much higher and worker capabilities lacking. Ronnie reiterated that this is our one shot to try to get it right: $280 billion to try to turn national security pejoratives into viable market economics. As part of President Trump's One Big Beautiful Bill, tax credits for semiconductor manufacturers building plants in the US will raise from 25 to 35%, in addition to continued threat of high tariffs for imported semiconductor [42].

With so much at stake, Americans deserve more public discourse and analysis of how our industrial policies are progressing and what we are learning from each misstep. Dani Rodrik is Professor of International Political Economy at Harvard Kennedy School. Dani is one of the few recognized thought leaders on industrial policy in America. When I spoke with him, he asserted that continued American technology primacy need not come by sabotaging Chinese technology development. While the Biden Administration has coined the phrase "small yard, high fence" to describe technology de-coupling with China, the small yard seems to get bigger and bigger, strengthening China's resolve to develop its own technology and exasperating America's global partners. In his paper titled "An Industrial Policy for Good Jobs," he noted that industrial policies have been with us for a long time, but often they have been carried out surreptitiously and without clear motivation. The recent revival of discussions around industrial policy provides a welcome opportunity for a thoughtfully crafted set of policies. A modern approach to industrial policy must respond to new circumstances. It must target "good-jobs externalities," in addition to the traditional learning, technological, and national security considerations. Relatedly, industrial policy's traditional focus on manufacturing and globally competitive industries has to be broadened to service sectors and smaller and medium-sized firms. We need to rely less on traditional top-down policy instruments—such as subsidies and tax incentives—and more on collaborative, iterative interactions whereby public agencies supply a portfolio of customized public services in exchange for firms undertaking soft commitments on the quantity and quality of employment [43].

After the Russian invasion of Ukraine, many friends decried to me the role played by the PRC, how it did not openly criticize Russia and instead continued to do business with it. I told them I shared their dismay, but what worried me more was why India, South Africa, Brazil, and some of the largest democracies in the world, did not take the stance of the Western democracies. In addition, 19 African countries abstained from the UN condemnation of Russian annexation of Ukrainian territories. When it comes to the interests and perspectives of the Global South, my fear is that the US has largely created an echo chamber of our own imaginings, without regard to realities on the ground [44]. In my travels across the globe, whether in speaking with the Argentinian Railway Minister on Chinese loans to build railways linking Vaca Muerta, a large oil and gas depository near Patagonia, or with a constellation of Latin American ambassadors to the Organization of American States (OAS) on China's growing significance as a trading partner, or just everyday citizens on the streets of Sudan or Tajikistan, my impression has been that diplomats and everyday citizens alike think China's investments a welcome opportunity, because they see tangible results and benefits.

The US is at risk of losing the Global South and along with it, the population and economic growth engines of the coming century. In 2021, President Biden, along with leaders of the G7 countries, announced the Build Back Better World (B3W) initiative [45]. Through B3W, the US and its allies hope to coordinate and mobilize private sector capital in four areas of focus—climate, health and health security, digital technology, and gender equity and equality—with catalytic investments from the respective development finance institutions. While at USAID, I had intense conversations with development experts on why the US and Western countries have largely stopped funding infrastructure projects in the developing world, and why China's attempt may augur differently. I was told that completing infrastructure projects in the developing world can be exceedingly onerous: the process is prone to corruption, lack of qualified local suppliers and partners, and recipient governments often have trouble repaying their debt. Indeed, China is now facing the same quagmires [46]. It persists because of its unique circumstances. China's foreign reserve, the largest in the world at $3.1 trillion, is mostly denominated in dollars and Western currencies. Its overseas investments in the Global South help diversify its risk and exposure to the West. Domestically, firms that have become the world's best at building railways and roads have increasingly fewer projects inside of China, and their capabilities and excess capacities are easily exportable. With geopolitical tensions with the West running high, a re-orientation of goods and services exports to the Global South benefits from local infrastructure buildouts. These and other factors determine that China's capabilities, risk tolerance, and long-term approach in the Global South are markedly different from that of the US and its Western allies. While it is commendable that the Biden Administration is re-focusing on the developing world, we should not copy China.

Of the four areas listed in the B3W initiative, digital technology deserves special attention. Across the developing world, digital technology and innovation are helping local populations leapfrog decade old development quagmires and inspiring young people to dream big and create the next unicorn, or a company valued over $1 billion. In 2023, I traveled with an investor group to Kenya and met with President William Ruto and US Ambassador to Kenya Meg Whitman. President Ruto specifically highlighted M-PESA, developed in 2007, that has become Africa's most successful mobile money service and the region's largest fintech platform. M-PESA provides service to more than 51 million customers across seven African countries who have mobile phones, but don't have bank accounts, or only have limited access to banking services. It has become the preferred way to send and receive money, top-up airtime, make bill payments, receive salaries, and get short-term loans for both the banked and unbanked [47]. President Ruto inquired how the US can facilitate more such breakthrough innovations for Kenya and Africa. Ambassador Whitman, who was formerly CEO of eBay and Hewlett Packard Enterprises, joked that when she first got the call from President Biden for the post, she asked why it couldn't be for France or Italy. But once landed in Kenya, she saw immediately the dynamism and pent-up energy of the local youth, and realized that her connections to Silicon Valley and expertise in digital technology are the best fit for the role.

Founded in 1997, and headquartered in New York City, Endeavor is the leading community of global high impact entrepreneurs [48]. Endeavor provides entrepreneurs, primarily based in the Global South, with services that help them grow ventures, create jobs, transform industries, and support future entrepreneurs. To date, the organization has supported over 50,000 candidates and selected over 2000 entrepreneurs from 1500 companies worldwide that have created over 4 million jobs. Endeavor alums such as Melvyn Lubega and Andrew Barnes co-founded Go1, a global reskilling platform based in South Africa. In 2021, Go1 became the first South African technology company valued at more than $1 billion dollars. I spoke with Allen Taylor, who leads Endeavor's efforts to connect its portfolio of more than 1500 high-growth companies with US-based mentors and investors. Since joining Endeavor in 2006, Allen has facilitated thousands of mentoring connections, and helped Endeavor companies raise more than $1 billion in equity capital. Allen calls Endeavor an engine for job and wealth creation, but also sees it as a role model for young people who want to dream big. Scaling a business is hard anywhere, entrepreneurs often toil in anonymity and are mired in challenges for a decade or more before breaking through. This is especially true in emerging markets. Allen is most proud of the fact that Endeavor has demonstrated that financial and economic successes are possible in the most difficult markets. When Endeavor first entered Brazil there were zero unicorns but now the country boasts 22 innovative companies with billion dollar valuations. Beyond capital, Allen notes that nothing is more valuable than creating human connections between Americans and their counterparts in the Global South. With innovative ecosystems having established in China, India, Brazil, and now emerging in Nigeria, Indonesia, the Middle East, and beyond, the US has a unique role to play to enable and benefit from the global digital revolution. Around the world, the US is no longer viewed as the builder of roads and railways. But we are still seen as the leader in innovation and breakthrough technology. In a world increasingly transformed by technology, we can improve local conditions, deepen local bonds, and create win–win partnerships through doing what we do best. Internationally, as domestically, our economic strategies must not be constrained by the faded glories of the past, but enlivened by the opportunities of the future.

References

1. Bloomberg (2023) US–China goods trade hits record even as political split widens. Available at: https://www.bloomberg.com/news/articles/2023-02-07/us-china-trade-climbs-to-record-in-2022-despite-efforts-to-split#xj4y7vzkg. Accessed 12 Aug 2025.
2. Bureau of Economic Analysis (n.d.) U.S. International Trade in Goods and Services. Available at: https://apps.bea.gov/international/factsheet/factsheet.html#650. Accessed 12 Aug 2025.
3. Federal Reserve Board (2019) US corporations' repatriation of offshore profits. Available at: https://www.federalreserve.gov/econres/notes/feds-notes/us-corporations-repatriation-of-offshore-profits-20190806.html. Accessed 12 Aug 2025.
4. Economic Policy Institute (2020) Growing China trade deficit cost 3.7 million American jobs between 2001 and 2018. Available at: https://www.epi.org/publication/growing-china-trade-deficits-costs-us-jobs/. Accessed 12 Aug 2025.
5. Autor D, Dorn D, Hanson GH (2013) The China syndrome: Local labor market effects of import competition in the United States. American Economic Review 103(6):2121–2168. https://doi.org/10.1257/aer.103.6.2121
6. Autor D, Dorn D, Hanson GH (2021) On the Persistence of the China Shock. Available at: https://www.nber.org/papers/w29401. Accessed 12 Aug 2025.
7. MIT News (2016) Trading places. Available at: https://news.mit.edu/2016/united-states-lost-millions-jobs-china-0309. Accessed 12 Aug 2025.
8. Bloom N, Handley K, Kurmann A, Luck P (2019) The Impact of Chinese Trade on U.S. Employment: The Good, The Bad, and The Debatable. Available at: https://pdfs.semanticscholar.org/18e3/7da77266333b2965010476a9d93fe8d4d4cd.pdf. Accessed 12 Aug 2025.
9. Stanford Center on China's Economy and Institutions (n.d.) Did the China shock cause widespread job losses in the US? SCCEI China Brief. Available at: https://sccei.fsi.stanford.edu/china-briefs/did-china-shock-cause-widespread-job-losses-us. Accessed 12 Aug 2025.
10. Oxford University Press (2016) Trade-induced technical change? The impact of Chinese imports on innovation, IT, and productivity. Review of Economic Studies 83(1):87–117. https://doi.org/10.1093/restud/rdv039
11. Stanford Center on China's Economy and Institutions (n.d.) How did open trade with China impact European firms? SCCEI China Brief. Available at: https://sccei.fsi.stanford.edu/china-briefs/how-did-open-trade-china-impact-european-firms. Accessed 12 Aug 2025.

12. National Bureau of Economic Research (2018) Re-examining the effects of trading with China on local labor markets: a supply chain perspective. Available at: https://doi.org/10.3386/w24886. Accessed 12 Aug 2025.
13. Autor D, Dorn D, Hanson GH (2020) On the persistence of the China shock. Quarterly Journal of Economics 135(1):1–48. https://doi.org/10.1093/qje/qjz020
14. Reuters (2025) China hits back at US tariffs with export controls on key rare earths. Available at: https://www.reuters.com/world/china-hits-back-us-tariffs-with-rare-earth-export-controls-2025-04-04/. Accessed 12 Aug 2025.
15. Harvard Kennedy School (n.d.) The Reimagining the Economy project aims to help build an economy at once productive and inclusive. Available at: https://www.hks.harvard.edu/faculty-research/policy-topics/globalization/reimagining-economy-project-aims-help-build-economy. Accessed 12 Aug 2025.
16. International Monetary Fund (n.d.) GDP at current prices, nominal GDP in U.S. dollars: China/United States. Available at: https://www.imf.org/external/datamapper/NGDPD@WEO/CHN/USA. Accessed 12 Aug 2025.
17. The Economist (2023) When will China's GDP overtake America's? Available at: https://www.economist.com/graphic-detail/2023/06/07/when-will-chinas-gdp-overtake-americas. Accessed 12 Aug 2025.
18. Harvard Kennedy School (2022) Edward Cunningham: What is the future of China's private sector? Available at: https://www.hks.harvard.edu/faculty-research/policy-topics/international-relations-security/what-future-chinas-private-sector. Accessed 12 Aug 2025.
19. CNN (2024) Evergrande, symbol of China's property crisis, heads to liquidation. Available at: https://www.cnn.com/2024/01/29/business/evergrande-ordered-to-liquidate-intl-hnk/index.html. Accessed 12 Aug 2025.
20. SSRN (2021) Mapping U.S.-China Technology Decoupling: Policies, Innovation, and Firm Performance. Available at: https://papers.ssrn.com/sol3/papers.cfm?abstract_id=3779452. Accessed 12 Aug 2025.
21. Stanford Center on China's Economy and Institutions (2022) Mapping US–China technology decoupling and dependence. SCCEI China Brief. Available at: https://sccei.fsi.stanford.edu/china-briefs/mapping-us-china-technology-decoupling-and-dependence. Accessed 12 Aug 2025.
22. Center for Strategic and International Studies (2025) DeepSeek, Huawei export controls and the future U.S.–China AI race. Available at: https://www.csis.org/analysis/deepseek-huawei-export-controls-and-future-us-china-ai-race. Accessed 12 Aug 2025.

23. Stratechery (2025) An interview with Nvidia CEO Jensen Huang about chip controls, AI factories and enterprise pragmatism. Available at: https://stratechery.com/2025/an-interview-with-nvidia-ceo-jensen-huang-about-chip-controls-ai-factories-and-enterprise-pragmatism/. Accessed 12 Aug 2025.
24. International Monetary Fund (n.d.) Cooperation for Recovery: The Marshall Plan. Available at: https://www.imf.org/external/np/exr/center/mm/eng/mm_dr_03.htm. Accessed 12 Aug 2025.
25. Council on Foreign Relations (2023) China's massive Belt and Road Initiative. Available at: https://www.cfr.org/backgrounder/chinas-massive-belt-and-road-initiative. Accessed 12 Aug 2025.
26. The Atlantic (2021) The Chinese 'Debt Trap' Is a Myth. Available at: https://www.theatlantic.com/international/archive/2021/02/china-debt-trap-diplomacy/617953/. Accessed 12 Aug 2025.
27. AidData (n.d.) AidData's global Chinese development finance dataset version 3.0. Available at: https://www.aiddata.org/data/aiddatas-global-chinese-development-finance-dataset-version-3-0. Accessed 12 Aug 2025.
28. Dolan CB, Malik AA, Zhang S, Mao W, McDade KK, Svoboda E, et al. (2023) Chinese health funding in Africa: The untold story. PLOS Global Public Health 3(6): e0001637. https://doi.org/10.1371/journal.pgph.0001637.
29. Economics Online (2020) Positive externalities. Available at: https://www.economicsonline.co.uk/market_failures/positive_externalities.html/. Accessed 12 Aug 2025.
30. Harvard Kennedy School (2022) The Reimagining the Economy project aims to help build an economy at once productive and inclusive. Available at: https://www.hks.harvard.edu/faculty-research/policy-topics/globalization/reimagining-economy-project-aims-help-build-economy. Accessed 12 Aug 2025.
31. New York Times (2025) Opinion | We Warned About the First China Shock. The Next One Will Be Worse. Available at: https://www.nytimes.com/2025/07/14/opinion/china-shock-economy-manufacturing.html. Accessed 12 Aug 2025.
32. Google (2021) Grow with Google and the Thurgood Marshall College Fund announce career readiness program for HBCUs. Available at: https://blog.google/outreach-initiatives/grow-with-google/career-readiness-hbcus/. Accessed 14 Aug 2025.
33. Council on Foreign Relations (2023) Is industrial policy making a comeback? Available at: https://www.cfr.org/backgrounder/industrial-policy-making-comeback. Accessed 12 Aug 2025.

34. Asia Society Policy Institute (2022) Assessing the scope, goals, and implications of China's Industrial Policy. Available at: https://fsi9-prod.s3.us-west-1.amazonaws.com/s3fs-public/2022-12/aspi_12.22.22_updated.pdf. Accessed 12 Aug 2025.
35. CSIS (2022) Red Ink: Estimating Chinese Industrial Policy Spending in Comparative Perspective. Available at: https://www.csis.org/analysis/red-ink-estimating-chinese-industrial-policy-spending-comparative-perspective. Accessed 12 Aug 2025.
36. Asia Society Policy Institute (2021) China's industrial policy: a roundtable summary report. Available at: https://asiasociety.org/sites/default/files/2023-01/ASPI_SCCEI_China%20Industrial%20Policy_%20Roundtable%20%20Summary%20Report_Final.pdf. Accessed 12 Aug 2025.
37. U.S.–China Economic and Security Review Commission (2011) Testimony before the US–China Economic and Security Review Commission. Available at: https://www.uscc.gov/sites/default/files/5.4.11Wolff.pdf. Accessed 12 Aug 2025.
38. RCR Wireless News (2014) RIP: China Mobile's TD-SCDMA 3G network. Available at: https://www.rcrwireless.com/20141217/carriers/td-scdma-3g-mobiles-td-scdma-3g-network-2009-2014. Accessed 12 Aug 2025.
39. McKinsey & Company (2022) The CHIPS and Science Act: here's what's in it. Available at: https://www.mckinsey.com/industries/public-sector/our-insights/the-chips-and-science-act-heres-whats-in-it. Accessed 12 Aug 2025.
40. CNN (2024) TSMC says its $40 billion chip project in Arizona faces a further delay. Available at: https://www.cnn.com/2024/01/19/tech/tsmc-taiwan-arizona-project-delay-intl-hnk/index.html. Accessed 12 Aug 2025.
41. Barron's (2023) Intel Delays Ohio Chip Plants. Slow Chips Act Funding Isn't Helping. Available at: https://www.barrons.com/articles/intel-ohio-chip-plants-b0beab90. Accessed 12 Aug 2025.
42. CNBC (2025) Chipmakers get larger tax credits in Trump's latest 'big beautiful bill'. Available at: https://www.cnbc.com/2025/07/02/chipmakers-get-bigger-tax-credits-in-trumps-latest-big-beautiful-bill.html. Accessed 12 Aug 2025.
43. Harvard Kennedy School (2022) An industrial policy for good jobs. Available at: https://drodrik.scholar.harvard.edu/sites/scholar.harvard.edu/files/dani-rodrik/files/rodrik_-_an_industrial_policy_for_good_jobs.pdf. Accessed 12 Aug 2025.
44. OSF Preprints (2022) Chinese State Media Persuades a Global Audience That the "China Model" Is Superior: Evidence From a 19-Country Experiment. Available at: https://doi.org/10.31219/osf.io/5cafd_v1. Accessed 12 Aug 2025.

45. White House (2021) FACT SHEET: President Biden and G7 Leaders Launch Build Back Better World (B3W) Partnership. Available at: https://bidenwhitehouse.archives.gov/briefing-room/statements-releases/2021/06/12/fact-sheet-president-biden-and-g7-leaders-launch-build-back-better-world-b3w-partnership/. Accessed 12 Aug 2025.
46. New York Times (2023) China Is Lending Billions to Countries in Financial Trouble. Available at: https://www.nytimes.com/2023/11/06/business/china-bri-aiddata.html. Accessed 12 Aug 2025.
47. Vodafone (n.d.) M-Pesa. Available at: https://www.vodafone.com/about-vodafone/what-we-do/consumer-products-and-services/m-pesa. Accessed 12 Aug 2025.
48. Endeavor (n.d.) About Endeavor. Available at: https://endeavor.org/. Accessed 12 Aug 2025.

CHAPTER 6

Human Rights: Our Values at Home and Abroad

Assumption 1: China should Become More like the US in Rights and Values
Assumption 2: America is Defending the International Rules-Based System
Omission: Our American Values Under Siege at Home

While I was interviewing for the President role at the Committee of 100, one Committee of 100 member and interviewer brought up the Hoover report, and said that it would be my responsibility to repair the damage. I took a mental note. Having gone to Stanford, I had biked past the Hoover Institution every day on my way to class. Located on campus at Stanford and in Washington D.C., the Hoover Institution is a conservative leaning think tank that focuses on the ideals of peace, individual liberty, free enterprises, and limited government. Its current director is Condoleezza Rice, Professor in Global Business and the Economy at the Stanford Graduate School of Business and former Secretary of State under President George W. Bush. Soon after taking the President role, while social distancing at home, I reached out to all 100 plus members of the Committee of 100 and with a few exceptions, spoke to all of them. Meetings after meetings, members brought up the Hoover report, and commented bitterly on perceived unfair attacks against the Committee. The report in question, published in 2019, is titled "China's Influence

Z. Z. Huang, *Rethinking China*,
https://doi.org/10.1007/978-981-95-3608-5_6

and American Interests: Promoting Constructive Vigilance." The report aimed to raise awareness of the PRC's efforts to penetrate and sway a range of American institutions: state and local governments, academic institutions, think tanks, media, and businesses. In particular, it highlighted aspects of the "discourse war" waged by the PRC government and CCP, including their view of Chinese Americans as members of a worldwide Chinese diaspora that owes undefined loyalty to the motherland [1]. The report referenced the Committee of 100 on several occasions, noting specifically that "the Chinese embassy also targets prominent Chinese Americans through the Committee of 100, an organization of the most elite Chinese Americans in the United States. Committee members report significant pressure from the Chinese consulate on Committee members to toe the Party line. Some prominent Committee members are openly sympathetic to the goals of the Chinese Communist Party. One of them is George Koo, who in addition to serving in a senior position on the Committee is also listed as an 'overseas director' of the China Overseas Friendship Association, based in Beijing."

This is code red for me. One, I did not want to represent an organization under the influence of any foreign government. Two, the Committee will have no credibility to pursue any of its missions if it is perceived as an organization under the influence of a foreign government. I reached out to the authors of the Hoover report, Larry Diamond, Senior Fellow at the Hoover Institution, and Orville Schell, Director of the Center on US–China Relations at the Asia Society. I sat down with Larry at the Stanford Faculty Club on a balmy California afternoon and spoke at length about his concerns. I shared with him what we are doing at the Committee. First, that we understand that the United Front has become a top national security concern for the US government. According to the Congressional Select Committee on the CPP, "United front work is a unique blend of influence and interference activities, as well as intelligence operations that the CCP uses to shape its political environment, including to influence other countries' policy towards the PRC and to gain access to advanced foreign technology. It is coordinated by the CCP's United Front Work Department and carried out by an extensive network of organizations and individuals operating in and outside of the United States, alongside the PRC's diplomatic and intelligence activities [2]." The Committee of 100 had worked with an organization based in China to facilitate its conferences and event planning in country (a requirement by the PRC government to organize large scale events in

China). After that organization was subsumed under the United Front Work Department, the Committee is now working solely with the American Chamber of Commerce in Shanghai as our local partner. Second, the member mentioned in the Hoover Report, George Koo, had resigned from the Committee. George believes firmly that as an American he has the right to speak his mind and that his connections to China are only to further US–China relations. But given the changing political landscape, he understands that the Committee cannot be seen as under the influence of any foreign government. Third, under my tenure, we are forthright with the State Department on our interactions with the Chinese or any foreign embassies. And fourth, insinuations and innuendos emanating from the report are unfortunately contributing to the rise in Anti-Asian hate and violence. Larry agreed that Chinese Americans have been loyal and contributing members of American society and that the report did not cast suspicion on the community as a whole. He denounced the rise in anti-Asian hate and violence and the irresponsible political rhetoric that have contributed to the upsurge. As an academic, he was especially concerned with the ill effects of the China Initiative, which drove talented individuals from academic pursuits in America. However, he quipped, just as I had heard in our meetings with the National Security Council and State Department, how the Committee can speak so forcefully on civil rights protection in America while being silent on human rights violations in China. I offered that if our common goal is national security enhancement balanced with civil rights protection, perhaps we can work on something together. On the issue of human rights in China, I had zero experience, but I am open to hearing his and others' thoughts.

Back at the Committee, I sought internal alignment. The members of the Committee of 100 are a diverse lot, many were born in mainland China, but many others were born in Taiwan, Hong Kong, and elsewhere. A large number are second-, third-, and sixth-generation Americans. Many speak Chinese fluently and have worked in China, but a good number only speak English and have visited China solely as tourists. When relations between the US and China were good, and engagement the official byword, Chinese Americans were highly prized for our ability to act as cultural bridges. Now that the vaulted buzzwords in Washington D.C. have moved away from cooperation to confrontation, how can we continue to serve our missions as an organization and community? We started town halls across the US to invite members to speak their minds. We conducted anonymous surveys so members can input their thoughts directly. We hosted a member retreat so members can sit in one room and debate face to face on how best to describe what we stand for and what we are willing to fight for. After a robust series of exchanges and discussions the members voted on the following language: "Committee of 100's members are American citizens who are proud of our contributions to the United States and our Chinese cultural heritage. We are an organization of Chinese Americans united by our belief in core American values and the fundamental principles of equality and fairness for all people, regardless of race, religion, national origin, gender, or creed. We support the full inclusion and advancement of the more than 5 million Chinese Americans in the United States and believe that America is stronger because of its immigrant heritage and diverse citizenry. We firmly reject all forms of prejudice, intolerance, and discrimination. We believe the well-being of all American citizens is affected by the US–China relationship and we encourage Sino-American dialog and cooperation whenever possible. We believe progress occurs when the peoples of the United States and China find common ground and work together to solve the world's most pressing challenges. We call on both governments and non-governmental parties to behave as responsible stakeholders and collaborate peacefully. We believe in a deeper mutual knowledge of the unique histories and cultures of the United States and China to foster mutual understanding and benefits. We are committed to supporting exchanges and cooperation between the two countries to this end, not least in the areas of: business, the arts, education, public health, science, and philanthropy [3]." I was heartened to see brilliant, thoughtful leaders with diverse backgrounds come together on these fundamental values for the organization. Yet on the topic of human rights in China, we were split.

A statement seemed necessary. But what should we say? As I polled our membership many good questions arose. "We are not human rights experts, what can we say?" "What are we attempting to achieve with the statement?" "Will our government trust us even if we release this statement?" "Why should we prove our loyalty when we have done nothing wrong?" "We are citizens of America, we are entitled to speak up against our government. But we are not citizens of China, what right do we have to speak up against the actions of another government?" "If we speak up and simply get cut off by the PRC government, what positive results would we have achieved?" "Will our speaking up change anything on the ground in China?" "If our mission is to facilitate constructive US–China relations, how will this help with that mission?" and many more candid and thought-provoking questions. I list these questions here because in recent years, American corporations and organizations have been asked to speak up on human rights violations in China, and my belief is that they too had to grapple with these and other difficult questions.

To better understand what standing we may have and how we may speak about human rights violations in a foreign country, I spoke to Sophie Richardson, China Director at the Human Rights Watch. Sophie first reached out to me when I started my tenure at the Committee of 100. As I had no experience in human rights work, she was very helpful in providing her thoughts and feedback. She spoke to me about the Uyghurs from Xinjiang who were persecuted, the protesters in Hong Kong who were jailed, and the activists—religious, political, or otherwise—within mainland China who were silenced. I told her about the set of values that the members of the Committee of 100 had agreed to that aligned with our American values and organizational missions. However, when it came to speaking about another country's human rights, applying American values seemed inappropriate. Countries' values are shaped by their unique history, culture, religious, and philosophical practices, and I wondered how we might apply our own values to another country. In fact, even within our own country, Americans debate vehemently over issues such as abortion rights, and it's impossible to say that either prolife or prochoice equals American value. Were there universal human rights or values that all countries subscribe to that we may lean on to speak out against human rights violations anywhere in the world?

Sophie paused and brought up the United Nations Universal Declaration of Human Rights. The Universal Declaration of Human Rights (UDHR) was spearheaded by Eleanor Roosevelt, wife of President Franklin D. Roosevelt, and adapted by the UN General Assembly in 1948. Although it's not a legally binding document in the traditional sense, and the words are sometimes flowery and vague, it sets out, for the first time, fundamental human rights to be universally protected. The UDHR is widely recognized as having inspired, and paved the way for, the adoption of more than seventy human rights treaties, applied today on a permanent basis at global and regional levels [4]. The UDHR preamble reads, and I share it here because like most Americans, I was vaguely aware of it but had never before read it: "Whereas recognition of the inherent dignity and of the equal and inalienable rights of all members of the human family is the foundation of freedom, justice and peace in the world. Whereas disregard and contempt for human rights have resulted in barbarous acts which have outraged the conscience of mankind, and the advent of a world in which human beings shall enjoy freedom of speech and belief and freedom from fear and want has been proclaimed as the highest aspiration of the common people. Whereas it is essential, if man is not to be compelled to have recourse, as a last resort, to rebellion against tyranny and oppression, that human rights should be protected by the rule of law. Whereas it is essential to promote the development of friendly relations between nations. Whereas the peoples of the United Nations have in the Charter reaffirmed their faith in fundamental human rights, in the dignity and worth of the human person and in the equal rights of men and women and have determined to promote social progress and better standards of life in larger freedom. Whereas Member States have pledged themselves to achieve, in co-operation with the United Nations, the promotion of universal respect for and observance of human rights and fundamental freedoms. Whereas a common understanding of these rights and freedoms is of the greatest importance for the full realization of this pledge. Now, therefore, the General Assembly, proclaims this Universal Declaration of Human Rights as a common standard of achievement for all peoples and all nations, to the end that every individual and every organ of society, keeping this Declaration constantly in mind, shall strive by teaching and education to promote respect for these rights and freedoms and by progressive measures, national and international, to secure their universal and effective recognition and observance, both among the peoples of Member States themselves and among the peoples of territories under their jurisdiction." While the PRC may disagree with certain aspects of American values, it is bound by its own commitment to the Universal Declaration of Human Rights.

Putting ideals into practice is invariably difficult. Sophie brought up a report on Xinjiang released by the Office of the UN High Commissioner for Human Rights (OHCHR) in late 2022 that concluded that "serious human rights violations" against the Uyghur and "other predominantly Muslim communities" had been committed [5]. She then shared with me a thought piece that she wrote that talked at length about how the PRC government is actively utilizing the UN systems to stymie human rights violation discussions [6]. The Freedom House, a Washington D.C.-based nonprofit founded in 1941 to defend democracy worldwide, reported that "the CCP and its proxies are using more sophisticated and coercive tactics to shape media narratives and suppress critical reporting. Mass distribution of Beijing-backed content via mainstream media, harassment and intimidation of outlets that publish news or opinions disfavored by the Chinese government, and the use of cyberbullying, fake social media accounts, and targeted disinformation campaigns are among the tactics that have been employed more widely since 2019 [7]." In Sophie's opinion, economic sanctions and international reproach have made scant difference. Only local activism has had any lasting impact. She seemed almost in tears when she confided that because of her work, she can no longer visit China, a country where she has many friends and which she loves dearly. I came away from the exchange with a much better understanding of the universal nature of human rights, but still curious as to how to effect human rights changes in foreign lands and cultures.

I sought out Andy Nathan, Professor of Political Science at Columbia University. Andy has dedicated his career to understanding and reforming human rights in China. He clarified that there is extensive academic literature about the place that human rights should occupy in American foreign policy. On the one hand, one may argue that human rights are a matter of principle and that the US government should advocate for it unwaveringly, whether against friend or foe. On the other hand, one may argue that international relations are complicated and messy, and that the US must be realistic and sometimes prioritize other considerations above human rights. In between, there is an argument that the US government should seek incremental and practical improvements, by low key action or private diplomacy if necessary. There is no one correct answer and only a perennial debate.

I asked Andy what constitutes human rights that are accepted and recognized in the US, China, and across the world. He demurred that the definition of human rights and values differ from place to place, culture to culture. He told me about his debate with noted scholars in China about political reform, human rights, and fundamental values as part of ten conversations between leading scholars in the US and China [8]. When I pressed him further, he, just like Sophie, referred to the Universal Declaration of Human Rights, a document that all 193 UN member nations have signed onto. He too rued that ideals are hard to actualize in real life, and that economic sanctions have largely been ineffectual in changing human rights behaviors in sanctioned countries. This has not stopped Congress from trying. The Hong Kong Autonomy Act was passed in 2020 by Congress following the PRC government's enactment of the Hong Kong National Security law. The Act imposes sanctions on officials and entities in Hong Kong as well as in mainland China that are deemed to violate Hong Kong's autonomy, and punishes financial institutions doing business with them [9]. The Uyghur Forced Labor Prevention Act was passed by Congress in 2021. It aims to stop the use of forced labor in the Xinjiang region and prohibits the importation of goods into the US that are manufactured wholly or in part with forced labor in the PRC [10]. In the 118th Congress (2023–2024), China remained a focus of legislative activity, with 376 bills introduced in just the first 9 months of 2023, and multiple new committees created that focus on China [11].

As I dug deeper, I found a consensus in academic literature that suggests economic sanctions don't change behaviors, and may prompt more human rights abuses in targeted countries. I connected with Amanda Murdie, Professor of International Affairs at the University of Georgia, who with colleagues in 2021 published a paper titled "Revisiting the Causal Links between Economic Sanctions and Human Rights Violations." In it, by tracking key human rights indicators such as freedom from political torture, killing, and imprisonment, she found that sanctions are likely to trigger domestic dissent, and this instability further induces the government to employ repression. Reduced government capacity caused by sanctions may harm the government's ability to screen and oversee its security agents, which would subsequently lead to increased human rights abuses [12]. Amanda shared that while it might feel good to hold targeted countries accountable for human rights violations through economic sanctions, research after research illustrate their limited successes and oftentimes adverse effects [13]. She opined that what seems to work is a combination of international awareness and shaming through shared values, alongside local mobilization. Private diplomacy by nature is difficult to track and quantify, but her research suggests a positive correlation between UN Secretary General visits and human rights improvements in host countries.

In Washington D.C. I have heard innumerable times that America had operated under the assumption that with economic liberalization, China would liberalize politically and become more like the US in human rights and values. Obviously, this has not happened. And practically, it may never happen. Instead of hoping that China may become more like the US, that it adopts American values and rights, it is more realistic to assume that China will follow its own trajectory, guided by its own internal politics and dynamics. Yet where the PRC falls short on human rights that it pledges to as part of the Universal Declaration of Human Rights and other international human rights treaties, the US, as a defender of the international rules-based system, has a responsibility to speak up and act. As Andy suggested, how the US chooses to act depends on answers to the manifold questions we should ask along the way: whether we seek to punish, to chastise, to effect change, or to pursue other considerations beyond human rights. We should stop expecting China to develop American values, but we should absolutely hold the PRC and ourselves accountable to the universal values that all nations have ascribed to as part of the international rules-based system.

While at Harvard Business School, I took a class with Professor Clay Christensen. He had asked us, what is the single most important thing that we can take away from 2 years at HBS? Some students answered with leading management theory. Others responded with stellar business network. While still others offered brilliant professors. He shook his head to all these answers. When the room was dead quiet, he imparted that if we had just learned to ask the right question, our 2 years of business education was well worth it. So, when I heard the statement over and over again, that America is defending the international rules-based system, I had to ask, "What is the international rules-based system, and can you give me some examples?" Invariably, there is a long pause since nobody really asks this question. But after some contemplation, experts within and outside the US government would give me the examples of World Trade Organization (WTO) for international trade, World Health Organization (WHO) for global health, and the United Nations (UN) for world peace and security. I use "international rules-based system" instead of "international rules-based order" (even though many authors use them interchangeably) because of the controversy around "order" being seen as non-legal norms set up for the benefit of select countries to the exclusion of others.

Unprompted, many would go into a soliloquy about how instead of defending the international rules-based system, some of our actions in recent years have actively undermined it. This is especially pronounced under the Trump administration, with actions such as blocking appointments to the WTO's seven-member Appellate body that rules over trade disputes [14], terminating America's relationship with the WHO [15], and cutting off funds to UN programs such as the UN Population Fund [16]. While the Biden administration has re-engaged with some of these international rules-based systems, it has invested more heavily in traditional and new alliances led by the US, including the Group of

Seven (G7), the North Atlantic Treaty Organization (NATO), the European Union (EU), the Trilateral Security Pact between Australia, the United Kingdom, and US (AUKUS), the Quadrilateral Security Dialog (QUAD), and the proposed Indo-Pacific Economic Framework for Asia. When I asked why the shift away from international rules-based systems, a constant answer was that the PRC has actively manipulated international rules-based systems, frustrating US attempts to call the PRC to account for its many perceived transgressions.

More than one hundred years ago, in the aftermath of the devastation of World War I, President Woodrow Wilson ushered forth a vision of a League of Nations, where nations around the world can gather to settle disputes and maintain peace. Unfortunately, the US Congress voted down American participation in the league. It took another World War, and President Franklin D. Roosevelt, to push for the establishment of the United Nations in 1942. The US further led the creation of the General Agreement on Tariffs and Trade (GATT), the predecessor to WTO, in 1948. Winston Churchill famously quipped that, "democracy is the worst form of government, except for all the others." The UN, WTO, WHO and other international rules-based systems are unwieldy and obstruse, but they are the only international rules-based systems that we have. The US is apt to lean on its allies for quick actions and specific programs. Yet without existing international rules-based systems we have no other bodies to coordinate with and hopefully prevent the next global pandemic. No other bodies with which to plan for and hopefully avert a global climate crisis. No other bodies through which to uphold and advance human rights common to all nations.

I spoke with Stuart Holliday, who served as United States Ambassador for Special Political Affairs at the United Nations from 2003 to 2005. His primary duties involved representing the US in the UN Security Council on issues including UN peacekeeping, sanctions, and counterterrorism programs. Stuart emphasized that the mission of the UN is to ensure that a World War never again happens. The UN is divided into the Security Council, with five permanent members, among which are the US, China, Russia, France, and Great Britain, and ten other members that rotate every 2 years. Permanent members have a veto on all UN decisions. There has been talk of adding additional permanent members, since the economic and political lots of France and Great Britain have fallen measurably since the end of World War II, while those of Japan, India and other have advanced appreciably. The General Assembly, which comprises the rest of the nation states, can pass resolutions but only Security Council rulings are binding as international law. Therefore, the General Assembly serves more as a court of international public opinion rather than a true global parliament with legislative powers.

Stuart commented that in certain American quarters the perception is that the UN is constraining American power and sovereignty. The UN has become unpopular because of the fear that rules passed at the UN could supersede American laws. As the US has become more skeptical of the UN, there is no confidence building with China to update or improve the international rules-based system. In Stuart's mind, we can either take our toys and go home or take leadership. Otherwise, China can rightly claim that the US wants it to play by the rules, but is itself leaving the game table. Stuart believes that there is a role for the UN. While recent focus has been on the inability of the UN to resolve regional conflicts in the Middle East or Eastern Europe, the UN has been remarkably active and effective in the areas of humanitarian aid, weather and meteorology, food security, public health, and IP coordination. UN organizations such as United Nations Children's Fund (UNICEF), United Nations Development Programs (UNDP), and Human Rights Council have become important international organs. UN humanitarian agencies help desperate people around the world. In Ukraine, where an estimated 17 million people need help, the UN refugee agency has provided cash assistance, housing and shelter. After the devastating earthquake in Turkey and Syria, UN convoys carrying food, water, tents, and medicine were the main lifeline for Syrians living in opposition held territories. In Afghanistan, UNICEF provides 15 million children with food and medical care. UNRWA, the UN body that cares for Palestinians, has been the coordinator and distributor of the aid crossing from Rafah, Egypt, into Gaza. 1.2 million Gazans, more than half of the number of people displaced, were sheltering at UN facilities [17]. In an international rules-based system, nations at once advance and subordinate their national interests. The question for America is, can we uphold the international rules-based system founded and led by the US in a multipolar world? There was a time when President George H.W. Bush built coalitions at the UN to secure the peaceful reunification of Germany and against Saddam Hussein following his invasion of Kuwait, today the choice is ours again on how America will continue to defend the international rules-based system.

As Congress continues to expand legislations to punish the PRC on human rights violations, Americans need to be aware of our own values under siege at home. On May 8, 2023, Florida Governor Ron DeSantis signed into law SB 264, which bars foreign nationals domiciled in China, Russia, Iran, North Korea, Syria, Venezuela, and Cuba from purchasing agricultural land or property within 10 miles of a military installation or critical infrastructure in Florida. The law also specifically bars any Chinese national from purchasing any real estate whosoever in the state, with limited exception for residential property by those with legal visas. In Missouri, Governor Michael Parson issued Executive Order 24–01 in January 2024, which prohibits the acquisition of agricultural land by Chinese, Iranian, Russian, and other citizens from designated adversarial countries within 10 miles of a military facility [18]. The Governor's press remarks focused almost exclusively on China: "With heightened concerns regarding ownership of Missouri farmland by foreign adversaries, especially China, we are signing this order to safeguard our military and intelligence assets, prevent security threats to our state, and give Missourians greater peace of mind." In terms of evidence that Missouri farmland has been exploited for nefarious purposes, Governor Parson declared that, "While we have had no issues yet, we want to be proactive against any potential threats… Believe me, if I had the authority, we wouldn't just be talking about banning farmland but all commercial properties by foreign adversaries… regardless of rural or urban [19]." In 2023, Arkansas became the first state to take an enforcement action against a Chinese property holder under new alien land laws. Attorney General Tim Griffin ordered Northrop King Seed Company, a subsidiary of Swiss company Syngenta (which in 2017 was acquired by state-owned China National Chemical Corporation) to sell its property as it was in violation of state law that bars a "prohibited foreign party-controlled business" from acquiring or holding land in Arkansas. Syngenta was also ordered to pay a $280,000 fine for failing to register with the Arkansas Department of Agriculture on time as a foreign owned entity. Northrop King Seed has owned the land in question, 160 acres in Craighead County, Arkansas since 1988. The land is used primarily for seed research specific to the soil type found in Arkansas [20].

As of July 2024, 151 bills restricting property ownership by foreign entities have been considered by 32 states (115 bills) and Congress (36 bills). Of the 151 total bills, 71 would prohibit Chinese citizens from purchasing or owning property, 12 were passed and signed into law in

Georgia, Idaho, Indiana, Iowa (2 bills), Nebraska (2 bills), Oklahoma, South Dakota, Tennessee (2 bills), and Utah [21]. As of June 2025, 14 states are considering 45 bills that would restrict foreign property ownership in some way while Congress is considering 15 bills. 25 states have passed 49 bills that restrict foreign property ownership, 17 of which passed into law in 2024, and 11 of which passed into law in 2025 [22]. In July 2025, the Department of Agriculture announced a plan to limit Chinese and foreign purchase of US farmlands for national security reasons [23].

All of a sudden, 1.4 billion Chinese nationals are automatically assumed to be agents of the PRC, with actions like buying a home or farm in the US equated with nefarious activities. Is there evidence of Chinese owned entities or individuals misusing American farmland against American national security interests? Sadly, no such data exists. As of December 2020, Chinese investors hold slightly less than 1% of foreign-held agricultural acreage in the US. In total, foreign investors reportedly hold interests in 2.9% of all privately held farmland in the US, meaning Chinese investors hold a grand total of 0.029% of American farmland [24]. Have there been Chinese spies caught near US military bases? The closest example is "suspicious" Chinese trying to visit US military bases [25].

In addition to Florida's SB 264, another law passed in Florida in 2023, SB 846, prohibits institutions from taking money from or partnering with entities in China and six other "countries of concern." The list of banned interactions includes offering anyone living in one of those countries a contract to do research. More than 280 faculty members at the University of Florida, which has the state's largest research portfolio, have signed a petition urging the university to clear up the confusion and to voice support for an open-door policy on hiring. "We urgently request a timely decision that allows us to recruit top international graduate students with an assistantship, irrespective of their nationality," declares the petition, "failure to act swiftly may result in the loss of exceptional students to other universities, and the damage will be irreversible [26]."

The first anti-Communist scare, or Red Scare, occurred between 1917 and 1920 in the US, precipitated by the events of World War I and the Bolshevik revolution in Russia. Laws such as the Espionage Act of 1917 and the Sedition Act of 1918 criminalized many forms of speech. The Sedition Act was the broadest with its criminalization of any disloyal language, whether in print or spoken, about the US government, notably its war efforts. Thousands of immigrants were accused of disloyalty and deported. A second Red Scare came with the revival of anti-Communist feeling after World War II that lasted into the 1950s. In Congress, the House Un-American Activities Committee was approved as a permanent committee in 1945 (it was abolished in 1975). Congress also enacted the Subversive Activities Control Act of 1950 and the Communist Control Act of 1954. President Harry S. Truman issued an executive order that mandated a federal loyalty program, and the FBI under Director J. Edgar Hoover compiled detailed information on tens of thousands of Americans suspected of being communists. Civil rights leaders such as Martin Luther King Jr. and others were closely watched and wiretapped by the FBI because they were believed to be agents of the Soviet Union [27]. Famously, Senator Joseph McCarthy, chair of the Senate Committee on Government Operations, brought numerous Americans before his committee to question their loyalty to the US and unsuccessfully investigated the armed services for Communist influences [28].

As the Red Scare intensified, America's political climate turned menacing. Elected officials from both major parties sought to portray themselves as staunch anti-Communists, and few people dared to criticize the questionable tactics used to persecute people suspected of radicalism. Americans also felt the effects of the Red Scare on a personal level, as thousands of alleged Communist sympathizers saw their lives destroyed. They were hounded by law enforcement, alienated from friends and family, and fired from their jobs. While a small number of the accused may have been aspiring revolutionaries, most others were the victims of false allegations or had done nothing more than exercise their democratic right to join a political party. Though the climate of fear and repression began to ease in the late 1950s, the Red Scare has continued to influence political debate in the decades since. In both periods, First Amendment rights guaranteeing free expression and free association were endangered and put on trial. The Red Scare is often cited as an example of how unfounded fears can compromise civil liberties [29].

Through commissioning the history of Chinese in America, I learned so much about Chinese American history, our trials and tribulations, and our and Asian Americans' determined efforts to achieve full citizenship in the country that we call home. More than one hundred years ago, similar alien land acts were passed in California, Washington, Oregon, Idaho, Montana, Arizona, New Mexico, Texas, Kansas, Louisiana, Missouri, Minnesota, Wyoming, and Florida. Then, the alien land acts targeted

Japanese and other Asian immigrants and forbid them from owning American farmland. Other additional state acts were passed that forbid Chinese from running businesses or entering into professions [30]. After war broke out between the US and Japan in 1941, all Japanese living in the US, regardless of citizenship, were sent to internment camps because they were believed, simply because of their ethnicity or country of origin, to be disloyal and untrustworthy.

Americans may disagree on many things. But I believe we all hold inviolate the Constitution as the foundation for our freedom and security. We all agree that we should not discriminate against someone simply because of where and how that person was born. It is not only American law but American value to say that a person should be judged on the basis of his character and actions, and not on guilt by association. The hysteria over China has hurt and is hurting American values. Already there are efforts within Congress to reinstate the China initiative. For example, the Commerce, Justice, Science, and Related Agencies Appropriations Bill, 2024—H.R. 5893 states that "since 2018, according to the Department of Justice, upwards of 80% of all economic espionage prosecutions brought by the Justice Department allege conduct that would benefit the Chinese state, and there is at least some nexus to China in around 60% of all trade secret theft cases. As the US engages with China in a geopolitical struggle unseen since the Cold War, it is vital that our agencies are laser focused on the threat at hand. This bill reverses the unwise decision to end the Justice Department's China Initiative…" [31]. At a time when America urgently needs men and women with the expertise to understand and meet the challenges and opportunities presented by the PRC, Chinese, and Asian Americans are systematically and selectively barred from serving in federal positions where they can be most helpful. The State Department has lifted 1400 assignment restrictions during the Biden Administration, but some 625 State Department employees still remain under the ban. Many Asian American diplomats and federal employees can recount being denied access or position simply because of their perceived ties to China or Asia [32].

In April 2024, Congress approved an extension of Section 702 of the Foreign Intelligence Surveillance Act. Congress first passed Section 702 in 2008 to target foreign terrorist organizations and individuals intending to do harm to the American mainland. Under Section 702, the National Security Agency (NSA) can intercept emails, phone calls, text messages, and other digital assets from non-Americans overseas. However, Americans who communicate with non-Americans could have their information swept up in the searches. Today, Section 702 has been repurposed to meet the objectives of increased competition between the US and PRC. For Chinese and Asian Americans, many of whom with family ties in Asia, this means that even as Americans, their information could be swept up, monitored, and scrutinized by the US government, without any privacy safeguards or due process. In fact, Professor Xiaoxing Xi was surveilled by the FBI in 2015 using Section 702 [33]. But potential abuse and misuse extend far beyond the Chinese and Asian American communities. The Foreign Intelligence Surveillance Court noted that the FBI had engaged in "persistent and widespread" violations of existing Section 702 query procedures, including improperly searching communications from 133 Black Lives Matter protesters and 19,000 donors to a congressional campaign around 2020 and 2021 [34].

Established by the 9/11 Commission Act of 2007, the US Privacy and Civil Liberties Oversight Board is an independent agency within the executive branch. The Board's mission is to ensure that the federal government's efforts to prevent terrorism are balanced with the need to protect privacy and civil liberties [35]. In a 2023 Report titled "On the Surveillance Program Operated Pursuant to Section 702 of the Foreign Intelligence Surveillance Act," the Board found that "Section 702 poses significant privacy and civil liberties risks, most notably from US person queries and batch queries... During calendar year 2022, approximately 246,073 non-US persons located abroad were targeted under Section 702... Except in the very limited circumstances covered by Section 702(f)(2) for certain FBI queries, government personnel are not required by Section 702 to make any showing of suspicion that the US person is engaged in any form of wrongdoing prior to using a query term associated with that specific US person. Nor does Section 702 require analysts or agents to seek approval from any judicial authority or other independent entity outside their agency... Americans' communications captured through surveillance can include discussions of political and religious views, personal financial information, mental and physical health information, and other sensitive data. Moreover, ordinary Americans may be in contact with Section 702 targets for business or personal reasons even if the Americans have no connection to, or reason to suspect, any wrongdoing by their foreign contacts and even when the government has no reason to believe the target has violated any US law or engaged in any wrongdoing [36]." Equal protection and privacy rights that Americans hold sacrosanct are under siege, and it is incumbent upon all well-meaning Americans to speak out.

The hysteria over China also hurts American economic interests in unplanned ways. In my conversations with entrepreneurs and high-net-worth individuals from China, many voice strong concerns over the direction of the PRC government and their asset protections within China. Many see the US as a safe haven to diversify their assets. People vote with their wallets. Whenever PRC capital control measures have loosened, money flows out of China, with a significant amount coming to the US. In 2018 alone, Chinese investors invested more than $30.4 billion in residential real estate in the US [37]. Many Chinese entrepreneurs have told me that overseas mergers and acquisitions is one of the few ways to get funds out of China. In the hysteria over China, we miss the reality that ordinary Chinese buy businesses and real estate in the US because they believe in the American dream, that it's a safer and better place for their assets over the long term. In our efforts to hold the PRC accountable for its human rights violations according to universal rights and values, we must not repeat the errors of our own past and let hysteria take hold in our own country. All Americans have a stake in ensuring that the excesses and tragedies of the past do not repeat themselves.

David Halberstam in his bestseller "The Best and the Brightest," examined the assumptions under which America entered the Vietnam War and clung steadfastly onto the illusion of victory despite mounting evidence to the contrary. Of the things he had not known when he started writing the book, he thought that "the most important was the degree to which the legacy of the McCarthy period still lived." The assumption that the Vietnam War was one between anti-communism and Communism blinded American policymakers—the best and brightest that our institutions had to offer—to the reality that it was really a struggle between colonialism and anti-colonialism. Furthermore, "among the top Democrats, against whom the issue of being soft on Communism might be used, and among the Republicans, who might well use the charge, it was still live ammunition." Today, the competition between the US and PRC is once again being billed as anti-communism versus Communism, and neither Democrats nor Republicans are wont to appear soft on Communists. The New Red Scare is not only hurting many thousands of innocent Chinese American scientists and Chinese immigrants, it also holds the specter of ushering us unwittingly into an armed conflict in detriment to our values and interests.

Better assumptions can be:

> Assumption 1: America is Defending Universal Human Rights
> Assumption 2: America is Defending the International Rules-Based System
> Assumption 3: America is Defending our Values at Home

The assumption that the US must act on human rights violations by the PRC is consistent with American values but merits debate on the most effective implementations. First, how can the US support and strengthen universal human rights and values, especially through international rules-based systems? Second, where economic sanctions may not produce sought after human rights changes, what other options may we employ? Third, beyond the US government, what can Americans and American institutions do to effect human rights changes in foreign countries? I came away from my deep dive in human rights convinced that Americans have a duty to speak out on civil rights violations in America, because this is our home; and the right to speak out on human rights violations anywhere we see injustices, because we are part of the human family. Yet as I have also discovered, speaking out on and effecting human rights changes in a foreign land is complex and nuanced, and each of us should also have the right to decide if, when, and how we may want to speak up.

On Oct. 4, 2019, Houston Rockets General Manager Daryl Morey tweeted an image that read "Fight for Freedom, Stand with Hong Kong." By the end of the weekend, Chinese officials had asked NBA Commissioner Adam Silver to fire Morey for his remarks. The League and the Rockets stood by Morey, citing his right to freedom of speech. China moved to stop showing Rockets games, and in February 2020, Commissioner Silver said the NBA could lose $400 million as a consequence of the fallout [38]. I talked with Committee of 100 member Derek Chang, who was CEO of NBA China at the time. Derek recounted that at the time he was working hard to ensure the safety of NBA employees based in Hong Kong given the ongoing protests. After Commissioner Silver confirmed the league's support for Morey, there was nothing to do except to manage the fallout, including an already planned shutdown of an NBA basketball academy in Xinjiang. The situation was made even more volatile when

American politicians and celebrities jumped into the fray, with Lebron James being pilloried for saying that Daryl Morey was "misinformed" before sending tweet about China and Hong Kong [39].

In 2023, after almost 3 years of internal discourse and debate, the Committee of 100 released its position on human rights: "Committee of 100 endorses the UN Universal Declaration of Human Rights and stands for the rights of all people to live peacefully, speak openly, and worship freely. We therefore call on all governments to embrace the political, religious, ethnic, and cultural diversity of their societies. It is that diversity which has fueled the dynamic, innovative, and resilient America of which Chinese Americans are an integral part and that we proudly call home [40]." As Chinese Americans, we can unequivocally speak to the diversity of America that has allowed us to make this country our home and contribute to its successes, and on that basis and the basis of the UN Universal Declaration of Human Rights I believe that we are on firm ground to speak out on specific human rights violations. Like the Committee of 100, other American organizations can play their own constructive role in promoting universal human rights and values. The US should not expect China to adopt American values, but we can and should defend universal human rights that all countries, including the PRC, have ascribed to.

One hundred years ago, without the US officially signing on, the League of Nations had no chance of surviving. International rules-based system needs defending, and no effective defense or reform is possible without the inspired leadership and active participation of the US. America should live up to our stated assumptions and actively defend the international rules-based system. I spoke with Ambassador Oh Joon, who was Ambassador and Permanent Representative of the Republic of Korea to the United Nations in New York from 2013 to 2016. He also served as President of the Security Council for May 2014. Oh had spent over twenty years in the UN system. Like Stuart, he highlighted the pre-eminence of the permanent Security Council members and their veto power. While there have been serious discussions on reforming the Security Council and the UN at large, it is not possible without the leadership and consent of the permanent Security Council members, in particular the US and China. He cited examples of the US and China working well together within the UN framework, notably the strengthening of UN sanctions against North Korea in 2017. Oh spoke of an implicit understanding among the permanent Security Council members that while they themselves are nuclear powers, such powers would be severely restricted from other nation states; and with a few exceptions such as India, Pakistan, Israel, and North Korea, the members have worked well together to enforce nuclear non-proliferation. That type of collaboration is broken today.

Charles Kupchan is a Senior Fellow at the Council on Foreign Relations (CFR) and Professor of International Affairs at Georgetown University. In 2021, he and former CFR President Richard Haass co-wrote an article in the Foreign Affairs titled, "The New Concert of Power: How to Prevent Catastrophe and Promote Stability in a Multipolar World [41]." His article drew inspiration from the period between 1815 and 1914 known as the Concert of Europe. During this period, the Great Powers of Europe maintained a balance of power and supported world peace. The parties—Russia, France, Great Britain, Austria, and Prussia—agreed to support each other in the event of war or internal conflict under the Treaty of Vienna. The Concert of Europe resulted in 99 years of relative peace in Europe [42]. During our conversation, Charles lamented that today, unfortunately, the Great Powers do not speak to each other on a regular and consultative basis, during which differences can be ironed out and some consensus arrived at. He believed that even with peer competitors who don't espouse democratic values, there are still opportunities to create measurable standards by which all parties are held accountable. Otherwise, we will continue to see mutual suspicions deepen and any minor incident may trigger an overblown response. As America gathers old allies and forms new alliances, there is much we can do, difficult as it may seem right now, to defend and enhance the international rules-based system.

Our defense of universal human rights will only be as effective as we defend our own values at home. We are all humans. Americans are not above panic or hysteria. However, American history has taught us that the times when we overreact—such as McCarthyism in the 1950s or racial profiling targeting Muslim Americans after 9/11—we have come to regret these episodes as un-American and worse, counterproductive to our stated national security goals. Noah Chauvin is counsel in the Liberty & National Security Program at the Brennan Center for Justice, where he focuses on issues related to government surveillance and emergency powers. Previously, he was intelligence counsel in the Office of the General Counsel in the Department of Homeland Security. Noah tells me that since Section 702's inception, *trillions* of pieces of communications by Americans and non-Americans have been collected. While Section 702 has provided foreign intelligence benefits, there is no evidence that reforms such as warrants for US person searches would compromise the benefits. In the past, overly broad powers derived from political hysteria easily led to targeting of minority groups and resulted in unnecessary harm to American values. On April 20, 2024, President Biden reauthorized Section 702. Senator Dick Durbin, the No. 2 Democrat in the Senate, objected, "If the government wants to spy on my private communications or the private communications of any American, they should be required to get approval from a judge, just as our Founding Fathers intended in writing the Constitution." His proposal requiring US officials to get a warrant before accessing communications of Americans failed to garner the necessary support, along with five other civil liberty focused amendments.

In June 2023, the Hoover Institution, in collaboration with the Asian American Scholar Forum, and the Committee of 100, jointly held an event titled "A Fresh Start: Safeguarding People, Rights, and Research amid US–China Competition" at Stanford University. Committee of 100 Chair, Gary Locke, joined Senior Fellows at Hoover Institution to discuss what went wrong in the US government's pursuit of IP protection, and how to work together to advance international scientific collaboration, uphold civil rights and liberties, and safeguard America's leadership in research, science and technology [43]. Through our work with the Hoover Institution and other conservative organizations, I have come to believe that Americans across the political spectrum can unite to defend our national security and protect our civil liberties. Only when we do so are we most effective.

In June 2023, the United States filed a Statement of Interest in Shen v. Simpson (N.D. Fla.), a lawsuit challenging provisions of the Florida law, SB 264. In the statement, the Justice Department declared that "the State of Florida recently enacted a statute that imposes new prohibitions on owning or purchasing land in the State. Among other provisions, Senate Bill 264 ('SB 264') prohibits individuals who are not U.S. citizens or permanent residents and whose 'domicile' is in China, or other so-called 'foreign countries of concern,' from owning or purchasing real property. The United States respectfully submits this Statement of Interest under 28 U.S.C. § 5171 to advise the Court of the United States' view that the provisions of SB 264 to be codified at Florida Statutes §§ 692.201–2052 violate the Fair Housing Act ('FHA') and the Equal Protection

Clause of the Fourteenth Amendment of the United States Constitution. These unlawful provisions will cause serious harm to people simply because of their national origin, contravene federal civil rights laws, undermine constitutional rights, and will not advance the State's purported goal of increasing public safety [44]." In a 2024 report to the Secretary of Agriculture, the USDA Equity Commission noted in its recommendations that, "historical racism and discrimination have led to exclusionary laws that restrict immigrants from owning US properties. The 1879 Oregon constitution specified that 'no Chinaman may own property.' In 1913, in response to anti-immigrant forces, California passed the Alien Land Law to ban Asian immigrants from purchasing properties including farmlands. Subsequent laws extended the ban to include US born children of immigrants and restrict land leases. Fifteen more states followed with similar alien land laws. It wasn't until after World War II that the US Supreme Court struck down these laws as unconstitutional. Today, fueled by anti-immigration sentiments, several states are considering alien land legislation to prohibit foreign nationals from certain Asian, Central American, and Middle Eastern countries from purchasing agricultural lands, under the guise of national security protection. Thirteen states have already passed legislations to prohibit Chinese foreign nationals from owning agricultural land or lands within certain distance of a US military instillation. Since their arrival, immigrants of color have been perceived as perpetual foreigners. These state proposals would put some communities, specifically Chinese, under unfair, discriminatory scrutiny and suspicion again. According to USDA data as of 2021, Chinese entities and individuals owned about 384,000 acres of U.S. agricultural land, less than 1% of all US agricultural land held by foreign persons. Thus, the attention and reaction to Chinese ownership of agricultural land is not a reaction to a real problem but can be better viewed as actions based on Xenophobic stereotypes [45]." Today, as history unfolds on the evolving US–China relationship, we have an opportunity to learn from the mistakes of the past, to not repeat the tragedies of one hundred years ago, and to live up to our values that our national security apparatus is precisely constructed to safeguard.

References

1. Hoover Institution (2019) China's influence and American interests. Available at: https://www.hoover.org/research/chinas-influence-and-american-interests. Accessed 19 Aug 2025.
2. U.S. House of Representatives, Select Committee on the CCP (2023) Select committee unveils CCP influence memo, "United Front 101". Available at: https://selectcommitteeontheccp.house.gov/media/press-releases/select-committee-unveils-ccp-influence-memo-united-front-101. Accessed 19 Aug 2025.
3. Committee of 100 (2023) Committee of 100—About Us. Available at: https://www.committee100.org/wp-content/uploads/2023/12/Committee-of-100-Fact-Sheet.pdf. Accessed 19 Aug 2025.
4. United Nations (1948) Universal Declaration of Human Rights. Available at: https://www.un.org/en/about-us/universal-declaration-of-human-rights. Accessed 19 Aug 2025.
5. United Nations News (2022) China responsible for 'serious human rights violations' in Xinjiang province: UN human rights report. Available at: https://news.un.org/en/story/2022/08/1125932. Accessed 19 Aug 2025.
6. Richardson S (2020) China's influence on the global human rights system. Available at: https://www.brookings.edu/wp-content/uploads/2020/09/FP_20200914_china_human_rights_richardson.pdf. Accessed 19 Aug 2025.
7. Freedom House (2022) Beijing's global media influence: Authoritarian expansion, power, and democratic resilience. Available at: https://freedomhouse.org/report/beijing-global-media-influence/2022/authoritarian-expansion-power-democratic-resilience. Accessed 19 Aug 2025.
8. Shirk S, Rozman G (eds) (2014) Debating China: The U.S.–China Relationship in Ten Conversations. Oxford University Press, Oxford.
9. U.S. Congress (2020) H.R.7440—Hong Kong Autonomy Act. Available at: https://www.congress.gov/bill/116th-congress/house-bill/7440. Accessed 19 Aug 2025.
10. U.S. Customs and Border Protection (2025) Uyghur Forced Labor Prevention Act. Available at: https://www.cbp.gov/trade/forced-labor/UFLPA. Accessed 19 Aug 2025.
11. U.S. Congress (n.d.) Congress.gov homepage. Previously available at: https://www.congress.gov/. Accessed 19 Aug 2025.
12. Liou, R., Murdie, A., & Peksen, D. (2021). Revisiting the Causal Links between Economic Sanctions and Human Rights Violations. Political Research Quarterly, 74 (4), 808–821. Available at: https://doi.org/10.1177/1065912920941596

13. Center for a New American Security (2019) When do economic sanctions work best? Available at: https://www.cnas.org/publications/commentary/when-do-economic-sanctions-work-best. Accessed 19 Aug 2025.
14. Reuters (2019) U.S. seals demise of WTO appeals bench—trade officials. Available at: https://www.reuters.com/article/trade-wto/u-s-seals-demise-of-wto-appeals-bench-trade-officials-idUSL8N28J3L6. Accessed 19 Aug 2025.
15. CNN (2020) Trump announces end of US relationship with World Health Organization. Available at: https://www.cnn.com/2020/05/29/politics/donald-trump-world-health-organization/index.html. Accessed 19 Aug 2025.
16. Council on Foreign Relations (2025) Funding the United Nations: How much does the U.S. pay? Available at: https://www.cfr.org/article/funding-united-nations-what-impact-do-us-contributions-have-un-agencies-and-programs. Accessed 19 Aug 2025.
17. New York Times (2023) On the Ground in Wars and Disasters, the U.N. Plays a Vital Role. Available at: https://www.nytimes.com/2023/12/05/world/middleeast/united-nations-war-gaza-israel.html. Accessed 19 Aug 2025.
18. Missouri Secretary of State (2024) Executive Order 1. Available at: https://www.sos.mo.gov/library/reference/orders/2024/eo1. Accessed 19 Aug 2025.
19. KMIZ ABC 17 News (2024) Missouri Gov. Mike Parson takes executive action on foreign ownership of farmland. YouTube. Available at: https://www.youtube.com/watch?v=G3ypfo6tDco. Accessed 19 Aug 2025.
20. Seed World (2023) Arkansas Forces Land Sale: Necessary or Knee-Jerk? Available at: https://www.seedworld.com/us/2023/10/27/should-china-own-u-s-farmland/. Accessed 19 Aug 2025.
21. Committee of 100 (2024) Committee of 100 Updates National Database Tracking Harmful Alien Land Laws Legislation. https://www.committee100.org/media-center/committee-of-100-updates-national-database-tracking-harmful-alien-land-laws-legislation-2/. Accessed 19 Aug 2025.
22. Committee of 100 (2025) Federal and state bills prohibiting property ownership by foreign individuals and entities. Available at: https://www.committee100.org/our-work/federal-and-state-bills-prohibiting-property-ownership-by-foreign-individuals-and-entities/?mc_cid=99a7a5fab3&mc_eid=55c6271732. Accessed 19 Aug 2025.
23. U.S. Department of Agriculture (2018) Farm security is national security. Available at: https://www.usda.gov/sites/default/files/documents/farm-security-nat-sec.pdf. Accessed 19 Aug 2025.

24. U.S. Department of Agriculture, Farm Service Agency (2020) 2020 AFIDA annual report. Available at: https://www.fsa.usda.gov/resources/economic-policy-analysis/afida/annual-reports/2020. Accessed 19 Aug 2025.
25. USA Today (2023) Suspected Chinese spies, disguised as tourists, tried to infiltrate Alaskan military bases. Available at: https://www.usatoday.com/story/news/politics/2023/05/31/suspected-chinese-spies-posing-as-tourists-discovered-in-alaska/70260712007/. Accessed 19 Aug 2025.
26. Science (2023) Florida law blocks Chinese students from state academic labs. Available at: https://www.science.org/content/article/new-florida-law-blocks-chinese-students-from-academic-labs. Accessed 19 Aug 2025
27. History (2021) Why the FBI Saw Martin Luther King Jr. as a Communist Threat. Available at: https://www.history.com/news/martin-luther-king-jr-fbi-j-edgar-hoover-communism. Accessed 19 Aug 2025.
28. Free Speech Center, Middle Tennessee State University (2023) Red Scare. Available at: https://firstamendment.mtsu.edu/article/red-scare/. Accessed 19 Aug 2025.
29. History (2019) Red Scare. Available at: https://www.history.com/topics/cold-war/red-scare. Accessed 19 Aug 2025.
30. LexisNexis (n.d.) Casebrief: Yick Wo v. Hopkins. Available at: https://www.lexisnexis.com/community/casebrief/p/casebrief-yick-wo-v-hopkins-1830540487. Accessed 19 Aug 2025.
31. U.S. House Appropriations Committee (2024) EXPLANATORY MATERIALS FOR THE COMMERCE, JUSTICE, SCIENCE, AND RELATED AGENCIES APPROPRIATIONS BILL, 2024—H.R. 5893. Available at: https://appropriations.house.gov/sites/republicans.appropriations.house.gov/files/FY24-CJS-Explanatory-Materials.pdf. Accessed 19 Aug 2025.
32. New York Times (2023) Asian American Officials Cite Unfair Scrutiny and Lost Jobs in China Spy Tensions. Available at: https://www.nytimes.com/2023/12/31/us/politics/china-spy-asian-americans.html. Accessed 19 Aug 2025.
33. Center for Strategic and International Studies (2023) Reforming Section 702 of the Foreign Intelligence Surveillance Act for the digital landscape. Available at: https://www.csis.org/analysis/reforming-section-702-foreign-intelligence-surveillance-act-digital-landscape. Accessed 19 Aug 2025.
34. U.S. Foreign Intelligence Surveillance Court (2021) Section 702 certification opinion. Available at: https://www.intelligence.gov/assets/documents/702%20Documents/declassified/21/2021_FISC_Certification_Opinion.pdf. Accessed 19 Aug 2025.
35. U.S. Privacy and Civil Liberties Oversight Board (n.d.) History and mission. Available at: https://www.pclob.gov/About/HistoryMission. Accessed 19 Aug 2025.

36. The Privacy and Civil Liberties Oversight Board (2023) Report on Section 702 oversight. Available at: https://documents.pclob.gov/prod/Documents/OversightReport/054417e4-9d20-427a-9850-862a6f29ac42/2023%20PCLOB%20702%20Report%20(002).pdf. Accessed 19 Aug 2025.
37. National Association of Realtors (2018) Profile of international transactions in U.S. residential real estate. Available at: https://www.nar.realtor/sites/default/files/documents/2018-profile-of-international-transactions-in-us-residential-real-estate-05-09-2019.pdf. Accessed 19 Aug 2025.
38. USA Today (2020) Today in 2019: Daryl Morey's Hong Kong tweet ignites firestorm. Available at: https://rocketswire.usatoday.com/2020/10/04/today-in-2019-daryl-moreys-hong-kong-tweet-ignites-firestorm/. Accessed 19 Aug 2025.
39. ESPN (2019) Daryl Morey was misinformed before sending tweet about China and Hong Kong. Available at: https://www.espn.com/nba/story/_/id/27847951/daryl-morey-was-misinformed-sending-tweet-china-hong-kong. Accessed 19 Aug 2025.
40. Committee of 100 (n.d.) About us. Available at: https://www.committee100.org/about-us/. Accessed 19 Aug 2025.
41. Foreign Affairs (2021) The new concert of powers. https://www.foreignaffairs.com/articles/world/2021-03-23/new-concert-powers. Accessed 19 Aug 2025
42. The Collector (2023) What was the Concert of Europe? Available at: https://www.thecollector.com/what-was-the-concert-of-europe/. Accessed 19 Aug 2025.
43. Hoover Institution (2023) A fresh start: Safeguarding people, rights, and research amid U.S.–China competition. Available at: https://www.hoover.org/events/fresh-start-safeguarding-people-rights-and-research-amid-us-china-competition. Accessed 19 Aug 2025.
44. U.S. Department of Justice, Civil Rights Division (2023) Shen v. Simpson (N.D. Fla.). Available at: https://www.justice.gov/crt/case/shen-v-simpson-nd-fla. Accessed 19 Aug 2025.
45. U.S. Department of Agriculture (2023) Equity commission final report. Previously available at: https://www.usda.gov/sites/default/files/documents/usda-equity-commission-final-report.pdf. Accessed 19 Aug 2025.

CHAPTER 7

Taiwan: The Avoidable War?

Assumption 1: Military Deterrence Is the Solution
Assumption 2: Defending Taiwan Is Defending Asia

The Book "2034," penned by Elliot Ackerman, former White House Fellow and Marine, and Admiral Jim Stavridis, former Supreme Allied Commander for NATO and four-star admiral, imagines a naval clash between the US and China in the South China Sea in 2034 that quickly escalates into nuclear strikes on the American and Chinese mainland. The nuclear exchanges destroy tens of millions of lives and reduce both countries to a shadow of their former selves. The book ends with a quote by William Faulkner: "Because no battle is ever won... They are not even fought. The field only reveals to man his own folly and despair, and victory is an illusion of philosophers and fools."

The possibility of an armed conflict between the US and PRC is real and increasing. American leaders speak openly of an existential struggle between democracy and autocracy, and almost all subscribe to the belief that military buildup is the best way to deter Chinese aggression in Asia, in particular towards Taiwan. At the same time, Chinese leaders speak openly of containment by America and likewise believe that military buildup is the best way to deter American intervention in Chinese domestic affairs. While both sides profess the logic of military deterrence to preserve peace, the reality is spiraling military buildups and

Z. Z. Huang, *Rethinking China*,
https://doi.org/10.1007/978-981-95-3608-5_7

a potential sleepwalk towards armed conflict. In the 2023 China Military Power Report submitted to Congress, the Department of Defense (DoD) described China as is the only competitor with the intent, will and capability to reshape the international order [1]. The report noted that China's military has focused on the rapid development of its nuclear, space, and cyberspace capabilities. DoD officials estimated that the Chinese had more than 500 operational nuclear warheads as of May 2023, and will likely reach 1000 operational nuclear warheads by 2030. It has the largest navy in the world, with a total battle force of 370 ships and submarines, including 140 major surface combatants. According to the report, "the People's Liberation Army (PLA) is aggressively developing capabilities to provide options for the PRC to dissuade, deter, or, if ordered, defeat third-party intervention in the Indo-Pacific region and to conduct military operations deeper into the Indo-Pacific region and globally."

The report also raised concerns over the risky and aggressive intercepts by China's military of US aircraft operating in international airspace. "Between the fall of 2021 and fall of 2023, the United States has documented over 180 instances of PLA coercive and risky air intercepts against US aircraft in the region—more in the past 2 years than in the previous decade... Over the same period, the PLA has conducted around 100 instances of coercive and risky operational behavior against US allies and partners in an effort to deter both the United States and others from conducting lawful operations in the region [2]." "The PLA's refusal to engage in military-to-military communications with the United States, combined with the PLA's increasingly coercive and risky operational behavior, raises the risk of an operational incident or miscalculation spiraling into crisis or conflict," quoted a senior DoD official on background [3].

The US is certainly not standing still. In his opening testimony before the House Appropriations Committee, Secretary of Defense Lloyd J. Austin III, flanked by Chairman of the Joint Chiefs of Staff, Mark Milley, requested a $842 billion military budget for Fiscal Year 2024, a 3.2% increase over Fiscal Year 2023 and 13.4% over Fiscal Year 2022 [4]. Austin noted in his prepared remarks that "this is a strategy-driven budget—and one driven by the seriousness of our strategic competition with the People's Republic of China... This budget includes a 40 percent increase over last year's for the Pacific Deterrence Initiative... This budget also makes the Department's largest ever investments in both R&D and procurement. We're requesting more than $61 billion to sustain our air dominance… We're also seeking more than $48 billion in sea power, including new construction of nine battle force ships… We're also requesting $11 billion to deliver the mix of long-range fires that our security demands—including major investments in hypersonics… And we've put forward the largest space budget in Pentagon history. We've requested $33.3 billion to improve our capabilities, our resilience, and our command and control in space… And we're asking for more than $30 billion to further invest in the industrial base and to buy the maximum number of munitions that American industry can produce."

American isn't alone in this build up. Austin observed that "the Philippines has agreed to nearly double the number of sites where we cooperate together… Japan committed to double its defense spending. And we're going to forward-station the 12th Marine Littoral Regiment—which is one of the most advanced formations in the Corps—in Okinawa so that we can better deter conflict in the First Island Chain… We've also made history with the AUKUS partnership. It's a generational initiative with our Australian and British allies to build game-changing defense advantages that will deter aggression, promote a free and open Indo-Pacific, and boost our defense industrial capability [4]."

The assumption in Washington D.C. is that military deterrence is the solution to both preparing for and avoiding war with China. Indeed, history is full of examples of military might deterring aggression, just as President Theodore Roosevelt had famously said, "speak softly and carry a big stick [5]." Yet history is similarly replete with examples of military build ups leading to armed conflicts, with World War I being a prime example [5]. Historians agree that when countries compete to build the biggest army, it creates rivalry and tension. When one country increases its military strength, its rival feels threatened and builds up in response. The military establishments begin to exert greater influence on public policy. All of this played out in Europe before World War I. For Germany and Great Britain, this meant a race for naval supremacy. Countries also form alliances. For Germany it was the Triple Alliance that included Germany, Austria-Hungary, and Italy. For Great Britain it was the Triple Entente which included England, France, and Russia. To illustrate the deep-seated mistrust that exist today between the US and PRC, on October 30, 2020 and January 8, 2021, Chairman Milley made two calls to General Li Zuocheng of the People's Liberation Army, his counterpart in the PRC, to assure him that the United States was not going to suddenly go to war with or attack China [6].

Taiwan today is talked about as the next Ukraine. All experts whom I have spoken to agree that Taiwan is the most likely flashpoint for an armed conflict between the US and PRC. The US media has reported timelines as early as 2025 [7]. The prevalent assumption is that the US can simultaneously avoid and prepare for such an armed conflict with the PRC, through strengthening our military, our military alliances, and equipping Taiwan's own defenses. With the election in 2024 of President Lai Ching-te of the Democratic Progressive Party in Taiwan, the likelihood for an armed conflict between Taiwan and the PRC seems higher than ever, and with that, the armed conflict between the US and PRC.

In one of my first trips to Washington D.C. as President of Committee of 100, I met a longtime friend of and consultant to the Committee, Marty Gold. Marty is a partner at Capitol Counsel LLC, a government relations firm based in D.C. While I was expecting him to educate me about the ins and outs of legislative work in Congress, he surprised me by confiding that his personal passion is US-Taiwan relations, which led to his publishing several books on Taiwan and the Taiwan Relations Act. He mused that the tension that we are now facing isn't new, in fact, it's been much worse before. The history of Taiwan is inextricably tied to conquests and empires. Dutch and Spanish settlers established bases in Taiwan as early as the seventeeth century. The island was annexed by the Qing dynasty in China in 1683 and ceded to Japan in 1895, as a result of the Treaty of Shimonoseki. The Republic of China (ROC), ruled by the Nationalists, began exercising jurisdiction over Taiwan in 1945 after the Japanese surrender at the end of World War II. After the Nationalists lost its civil war against the Communists, around 1.2 million people relocated from China to Taiwan along with the ROC government in the late 1940s and early 1950s. Since then, the Republic of China (Taiwan's official name) has continued to exercise effective jurisdiction over the main island of Taiwan and a number of outlying islands, leaving Taiwan and mainland China each under the rule of a different government [8].

Since the founding of the PRC in 1949, there have been four Taiwan Strait crises. The first crisis occurred in 1954, when PRC troops bombed Taiwan ruled Kinmen and Matsu, two small islands just a few miles from the mainland, and successfully captured Yijiangshan Islands. The second crisis occurred in 1958 with renewed PRC bombardments of Kinmen and Matsu and physical clashes near the Dongding islands. In response, President Eisenhower ordered American military to escort and re-supply Taiwanese supply lines. In both instances the PRC and Taiwan were in direct military conflict and the US came perilously close to armed conflict with the PRC, with nuclear options being considered. Eventually, the PRC and Taiwan arrived at an arrangement, in which they shelled each other's garrisons on alternate days. This continued for twenty years until the PRC and the US normalized relations [9]. The third crisis occurred in 1995 when PRC test fired missiles around Taiwan to protest Taiwanese President Lee Teng Hui's visit to the US. And the fourth and latest crisis occurred as a response to Speaker of the House Nancy Pelosi's visit to Taiwan in 2022, unleashing the largest ever PRC military exercise around Taiwan.

Since the re-normalization of US–China relations in 1972, not only the US and China have enjoyed a period of almost unprecedented engagement and shared economic growth, Taiwan and China have enjoyed a similar period of unprecedented engagement and shared economic growth. In fact, from zero economic interaction in 1972, China is now Taiwan's largest trading partner by far, accounting for 42% of Taiwanese exports, versus 15% for the US [10]. In addition, 70,000 Taiwanese manufacturers have set up facilities in China. In 2022, China accounted for 22.6% of Taiwan's total trade and 19.6% of its imports. That same year, the value of cross-strait trade between Taiwan and China was $205.11 billion. Between 1991 and the end of 2022, Taiwan had approved $203.33 billion of investments in China [11].

I connected with Shelley Rigger, Professor of Asian Politics at Davidson, who chronicled in her book "The Tiger Leading the Dragon," the significant role that Taiwanese entrepreneurs and firms played in the economic growth of China since 1978. Shelley believed that there would be no Chinese economic miracle of the last forty years without Taiwanese involvement. Starting in the late 1980s, Taiwanese businesspeople moved their manufacturing facilities to China and brought with them capital, manufacturing and management expertise, and most importantly, international clientele. Starting in plastics, toys and apparels, the move accelerated to information and communications technologies. In 2008, Taiwanese firms operating in mainland China employed around 15 million workers and accounted for around 4% of the country's tax receipts. Taiwanese firm Foxconn remains the largest private employer in

China and Taiwan is the second largest source of foreign direct investment (FDI) in China, after only Hong Kong.

In the 1980s, the Personal Computer (PC) revolution took off in the US, contributing to and benefiting from the outsourcing of PC manufacturing to Taiwan. Soon after, Taiwanese Original Design Manufacturers (ODMs) moved en masse to China to setup factories. When I moved to China on behalf of Intel in 2005, I frequented Taiwan because most of the PC and cell phone ODMs were then headquartered in Taiwan, with manufacturing in China. In Shanghai, I stayed in an area called Gubei in Hongqiao District, colloquially known as Little Taipei because of the large number of Taiwanese businesspeople who lived there. Perhaps it is these enduring ties that help explain why, strangely, despite the high tensions and threat of imminent war, most Taiwanese I have spoken to don't seem to be overly concerned [12].

To understand more I met with representatives of the Taipei Economic and Cultural Representative Office (TECRO) for lunch in Washington D.C. Because Taiwan is not recognized as a sovereign nation by the majority of countries, including the US, Taiwan does not have embassies but instead TECROs in host countries. Our lunch had taken place the week that President Tsai Ing Wen of Taiwan was visiting the US, amid reports of high tension and potential conflict in the Taiwan Straits [13]. The Committee of 100 is one of few American organizations that maintains friendly relations with the administrations in mainland China, Hong Kong, and Taiwan. In previous years, when the Committee of 100 had led delegations to Asia, it had always met with top leaders in mainland China, Hong Kong, and Taiwan. In fact, a good number of Committee of 100 members are based in Taiwan, with significant businesses on the island. Morris Chang, the founder of Taiwan Semiconductor Manufacturing Company (TSMC), was a long-time member until he resigned during the COVID-19 pandemic. Steven Chen, the founder of YouTube, moved to Taiwan to invest in the local startup ecosystem.

After we reviewed the long years of exchange and friendly relations between Taiwan and the Committee of 100, after my sharing my many visits to Taiwan and my observation that Taiwan has contributed mightily to the economic miracle in China, I asked how people in Taiwan felt about the rising tensions and potential for war. "We are very concerned that we are caught between the rivalry of two great powers, Mr. Huang." The answer startled me. Over the next hours I began to understand. Taiwan has no chance of self-defense, either in a naval blockade or amphibious invasion by the PRC, without direct military intervention by the US. The Taiwanese population of 24 million is smaller than the 29 million people who live in the city of Shanghai alone. Its GDP of $762 billion is comparable to that of Shanghai alone. Experts agree that any amount of defense spending and military preparation that Taiwan adds on is simply to prolong the time needed until the US can come to its aid. Living with the contradictions of increased PRC military and diplomatic pressures [14], rising political tensions between the US and PRC, continuing cross-strait economic and cultural relations, and a growing sense of independence and nationhood [15], the majority of Taiwanese feel resigned to being caught between two rival superpowers, their destiny both within and outside of their control.

From Marty I learned that under the Taiwan Relations Act, the US is not obligated by law to militarily defend Taiwan. Instead, the Act directs "the President to inform the Congress promptly of threats to the security or the social or economic system of the people on Taiwan, and any danger to the United States interests arising from such threats. It specifies that the President and the Congress shall determine the appropriate action in response to any such danger [16]." This is what is commonly referred to as strategic ambiguity: the PRC won't invade because it believes that the US may intervene militarily, and Taiwan won't declare independence because it is not certain that the US will intervene militarily [17]. Yet if the PRC were to invade Taiwan, how would an armed conflict between the PRC and Taiwan, and between the PRC and US look like? I spoke to numerous experts at the intersection of US-Taiwan relations and defense strategy.

As the wars in Ukraine and elsewhere have vividly demonstrated, war is unpredictable, and the costs of war oftentimes far exceed expectations. The US government runs classified war games on Taiwan but only a few public ones have been conducted by reputable organizations [18]. Nobody can predict how an armed conflict between the PRC and US will play out exactly, but there seems to be definite escalation points that either side must decide to respond to. My conversations with security experts always start with their pointing out the enormous economic costs to be borne by the PRC in case of an armed conflict. This is very understandable in light of the economic sanctions enacted towards Russia after the Ukrainian invasion. It is reasonable to assume that if the PRC were to invade Taiwan militarily, the US and its allies would enact significant economic sanctions towards the PRC. What is not clear, and perhaps impossible to predict, given the intertwined economic relationships between the PRC and the US and its allies, is the economic costs to the US and its allies. Furthermore, given how much Russia has been able to withstand Western economic sanctions in the short term, and how quickly Europe has moved away from Russian oil and gas, it is not clear that economic costs would do anything to stop an armed conflict once it has commenced.

If the situation deteriorates to such a point that supposed economic costs are no longer a deterrent, experts typically see the first escalation point, short of direct military confrontation, to be a military blockade of Taiwan by the PRC. Given that Taiwan is an island largely dependent on resources from the outside, an economic blockade would be devastating to its economy. The second escalation point would be a direct invasion of Taiwan by the PRC. A significant difference between Russia and Ukraine, and the PRC and Taiwan, is that there will be no proxy war ala Ukraine, where the US can simply provide military equipment, financial support, and intelligence and training without putting American lives at stake. Taiwan simply cannot defend itself against the PRC without direct American military intervention. The third escalation point is direct US and PRC military confrontation on the oceans and in and around Taiwan. Estimates vary but it is reasonable to assume that ships, airplanes, and many lives will be lost on both sides. The fourth escalation point is the targeting of military bases and installations on both sides. The PRC military bases and installations because they are where the PLA keeps its warships and long-range missiles. The American military bases and installations because they are the forward stations for American aircrafts, ships, and supply lines. The targeting of American military bases in allied countries will likely bring allies such as Japan into the armed conflict. The fifth escalation point is casualties to civilian areas and civilians. As experts point out, relevant PRC military bases are located on China's eastern seaboard, where population centers are close by and civilian casualty unavoidable. American military bases are also stationed in American territories such as Guam. The escalation discussions usually end there because if Chinese cities are bombed, and US overseas military bases and civilian areas are destroyed, the next escalation points, involving the American mainland and nuclear weapons, become too catastrophic and devastating to contemplate.

I connected with Michael Swaine, Senior Research Fellow at Quincy Institute for Responsible Statecraft. For nearly two decades, Michael had directed, along with Iain Johnston of Harvard University, a multi-year crisis prevention project with partners in China. When I shared with him what I had learned from various experts, he countered that escalation points are reasonable in theory, but once armed conflict commences, it is incredibly difficult to manage escalations. For example, a naval blockade may sound less destructive, but if the US were to break the blockade, an armed conflict may quickly ensue.

In 2023, the Center for Strategic and International Studies (CSIS) conducted one of the few public war games on Taiwan called "The First Battle of the Next War [18]." I quote the report at length below to illuminate the consequences of war. "The invasion always starts the same way: an opening bombardment destroys most of Taiwan's navy and air force in the first hours of hostilities. Augmented by a powerful rocket force, the Chinese navy encircles Taiwan and interdicts any attempts to get ships and aircraft to the besieged island. Tens of thousands of Chinese soldiers cross the strait in a mix of military amphibious craft and civilian roll-on, roll-off ships, while air assault and airborne troops land behind the beachheads… However, in the most likely "base scenario," the Chinese invasion quickly founders. Despite massive Chinese bombardment, Taiwanese ground forces stream to the beachhead, where the invaders struggle to build up supplies and move inland. Meanwhile U.S. submarines, bombers, and fighter/attack aircraft, often reinforced by Japan Self-Defense Forces, rapidly cripple the Chinese amphibious fleet. China's strikes on Japanese bases and U.S. surface ships cannot change the result: Taiwan remains autonomous."

This defense comes at a high cost. In the base scenario, "the United States lost between 168 and 372 aircraft. Subtracting the 96 Navy fighter/attack aircraft lost on US aircraft carriers in all base scenario iterations, the Air Force suffered losses between 70 and 274 aircraft, mostly on the ground… In all iterations of the base scenario, US Navy losses included two US aircraft carriers as well as between 7 and 20 other major surface warships (e.g., destroyers and cruisers) … Taiwan's air losses included roughly half of its operational air force, the majority lost on the ground to missile strikes. Even within the scope of these relatively short iterations, the 26 ships of Taiwan's navy (22 frigates and 4 destroyers) were destroyed by a combination of China's joint fire strikes and aggressive hunting by China's second-tier naval ships. The land battles were fierce but limited in scale, with Taiwanese army casualties averaging about 3500, with about a third of those killed."

China's losses in the base scenario were also high. In all iterations, PLA Navy ships around Taiwan were the primary focus of attack, and China's naval losses averaged 138 major ships in the three iterations of the base scenario. On average, these included 86 amphibious ships (90 percent of the total) and 52 other major surface warships. 244 Chinese aircraft losses, averaging 161 fixed-wing combat aircraft per iteration, were smaller than those for the United States... China's overall personnel losses were high. In ground combat, China suffered an average of 7 battalion-equivalents destroyed, equal to Taiwan's ground losses. This would translate to about 7000 casualties, roughly a third of whom are assumed killed. Another roughly 15,000 soldiers were lost at sea, with half assumed killed. Finally, many (and probably an overwhelming majority) of the 30,000-plus Chinese survivors on Taiwan would likely become prisoners at the end of combat.

Victory is not everything. The United States might win a pyrrhic victory, suffering more in the long run than the "defeated" Chinese. A conflict with China would be fundamentally unlike the regional conflicts and counterinsurgencies that the United States has experienced since World War II, with casualties exceeding anything in recent memory. Further, the casualty calculations shown in this report, as high as they are, do not encompass the full scope of the war. They cover only the first three or four weeks of the conflict and exclude casualties arising from the battles in the South China Sea, which the wargame abstracted. Thus, numbers presented here represent a floor, not a ceiling. During the height of the wars in Iraq and Afghanistan, the United States sustained about three killed per day. At the height of the Vietnam War, in 1968, the United States lost 30 killed per day. The loss rate here, about 140 per day in the base case, approaches that of World War II, 300 killed per day. Deaths (vs. casualties, which includes wounded) in three weeks of combat around Taiwan (about 3200) are about half the total from 20 years of combat in Iraq and Afghanistan (5474).

Taiwan's economy would be debilitated: Chinese forces, even if defeated, would inflict massive damage on Taiwanese infrastructure and cripple its economy for many years. Both Taiwan and the United States might suffer damage to civilian and economic infrastructure... The United States would suffer tremendous damage to its military forces. Rebuilding these capabilities would take many years and would occur at a slower rate than China's rebuild, given the rapid pace of Chinese military modernization. With only two US shipyards currently building large surface combatants, it would take decades to replace the dozen or more such ships lost while continuing the Navy's build program. Lost carriers could not be replaced because the current shipyard capacity is sufficient only to maintain the current carrier

> force. Aircraft would be a bit easier to replace. 334 Ships and aircraft would take longer to replace if the war went beyond the three or four weeks of game play or if losses from engagements in the South China Sea were calculated and included.
> The world would not be standing still during and after a US–China conflict. Other countries – for example, Russia, North Korea, or Iran – might take advantage of US distraction to pursue their agendas. After the war, a weakened US military might not be able to sustain the balance of power in Europe or the Middle East... Although this project focused on conventional conflict, many analyses of an invasion have nuclear play... The CNAS wargame, Dangerous Straits, similarly ends with the use of nuclear weapons. No one knows what those escalation dynamics would be. They depend on an unprecedented event, conventional war between nuclear powers... These losses might cause strategic disillusionment. The United States would sustain as many personnel casualties in a month of such conflict as in 20 years of wars in Iraq and Afghanistan. The scale and suddenness of such losses would shock a US population unaccustomed to significant military losses... Finally, the war might not end after this initial phase but drag on for months or even years. Conflict might be episodic, with periodic ceasefires...

I spoke with the authors of the war game, Eric Heginbotham, Principal Research Scientist for the Center for International Studies at MIT and Mark Cancian, Senior Researcher at the Naval War College. Both reaffirmed the heavy costs of war for all sides, in particular for China. Both highlighted that the chances of escalation are high if civilian casualties mount, and the war may widen to include allies such as Japan if American bases in Japan are attacked. Much of the success of the first battle will hinge on the Taiwanese being able to hold the beachhead until American reinforcements arrive. Like Eric and Mark, experts usually, not always, conclude that the US will win the battle for Taiwan based on military superiority. In return, I always ask, "if we win the battle, what about the war?" If the PRC is committed to reclaim Taiwan militarily, despite the immense economic and human costs, even after it suffers a military defeat, will it stop? Will winning the battle mean the end of the war? Here all experts raise the notion of *will*. Does America have the will to engage in long-term military conflict with the PRC? Nobody knows the answer but there is a historical precedent. In 1950, the newly established PRC, without a navy or air force, under the threat of nuclear bombardment by the sole nuclear superpower at the time, entered the Korea War in direct confrontation against the US. The economic and human costs to the PRC were immense, but it fought the US to a standstill. After three years, an armistice between North and South Korea was signed that still stands today. Losing the war on Taiwan may be existential to the PRC, is it to the US? Some experts lament that time may be on the PRC's side, given that the Taiwan strait is in its backyard and that the lessons of Afghanistan, Iraq, and increasingly Ukraine teach a potential adversary to simply wear America down. Michael Swaine holds a different view. He believes that in order to demonstrate American will or resolve, the US may escalate forcibly and rapidly, especially when American military and civilian casualties are involved. What results will be unpredictable and potentially catastrophic for all sides.

No one can predict how a war between the US and PRC will end. But it seems clear to me that there will be no obvious winner but real losers in Taiwan, China, and the US. Taiwan will suffer irreparably not only because of the devastations of war, but because as long as war continues, Taiwan will not be able to recover. Already, Taiwanese entrepreneurs have complained to me that foreign companies are not investing in Taiwan today for fear of potential armed conflict down the road. It is morbidly logical, why would a foreign company invest in a potential war zone? China will lose because it will meet a foe with the world's finest military, honed by decades of war and backed by industrial and technological might. Even if China takes over Taiwan, the ensuing economic isolation and devastation will likely set back its economic and social agendas for many decades to come. The US will not only lose significant American lives and treasures, but will likely put its entire Asian portfolio in jeopardy. To see defending Taiwan as a military problem alone is shortsighted and dangerous at worst. Perhaps war is unavoidable. But there must be a better solution, or at least attempts to seek out a better solution, for the sake of American lives at home and interests abroad.

But why intervene militarily at all? I questioned experts both within and outside the US government. The uniform first response is that Taiwan is a long-time ally and a shining beacon of democracy in Asia. We have to defend it. I counter that there are other democracies under threat around the world. For example, we left a democratically elected Afghanistan that we spent decades and trillions of dollars supporting, even though we knew that it could not defend itself against the Taliban. Why Taiwan in particular when the costs seem so high? After some consideration, the consistent answer is that if America does not defend Taiwan, our security guarantees and alliances in Asia, with South Korea, Japan, among others, will be viewed as unreliable. Not defending Taiwan would deal a significant loss of American credibility in Asia, and mark the likely retrenchment of American influence and power in the region. From a geopolitical perspective, as Assistant Secretary of Defense Ely Ratner had noted, "Taiwan is located at a critical node within the first island chain, anchoring a network of US allies and partners—stretching from the Japanese archipelago down to the Philippines and into the South China Sea—that is critical to the region's security and critical to the defense of vital US interests in the Indo-Pacific." Without Taiwan, the PRC will struggle to project power far beyond China's shores. However, if the PRC were to annex Taiwan and its military assets, it will be able to limit the US military's operations in the region and its ability to defend its Asian allies. With Taiwan under PRC's control, the US would have a far more difficult task to maintain a balance of power or to prevent a PRC bid for regional dominance [19]. By not defending Taiwan, America may be ceding Asia to the PRC. Taiwan is really a chess piece in the larger chessboard of Asia, and the evolving roles of the US and PRC in the region.

In 2009, the PRC offered a "Nine-Dashed Line" claim in the South China Sea. In 2016, in a unanimous decision, an Arbitral Tribunal constituted under the 1982 Law of the Sea Convention rejected much of the PRC's South China Sea claims. However, the State Department records that the PRC continues to use intimidation to bully Southeast Asian coastal states out of offshore resources, threaten them out of shipping lanes, assert unilateral dominion, and deprive fishermen of access [14]. In response, the US has stepped up its freedom of Navigation Operations. On October 22, 2023: A collision between two coast guard vessels from the US and PRC. On October 26, 2023: A Chinese jet fighter closes in on a US B-52 aircraft over the South China Sea. On January 4, 2024: The PRC and the US hold rival military drills in the South China Sea. A war in and around Taiwan can easily spill over to the South China Sea. I asked this question to a former US cabinet member well versed in US–China relations. Her answer gravely concerned me. She said that the thought keeps her up at night. The thought that we might sleepwalk into an armed conflict in Taiwan that will not only cost significant American lives and treasures over an extended period of time, but that may presage the total loss of American influence in Asia.

Better assumptions can be:

Assumption 1: Deterrence for Diplomacy
Assumption 2: Enhancing and Integrating American Economic Interests in Asia

Whenever I inquire about a better solution to war, silence ensues. The silence is broken by the unvarying declaration that this is why we must build up our military to deter Chinese aggression. Whenever I inquire what an equilibrium state that meets the interests of the US, Taiwan, and China might look like, I get silence and blank stares from experts. Then I had a meeting with Stapleton Roy, former US ambassador to China, who had worked with Henry Kissinger and others during the period leading up to the re-normalization of relations between the US and China. Two things that he cited intrigued me. First, he said that more than fifty years ago, visionary leaders on both sides came up with a story, made up purely of fiction, that met the needs of the times. That story, that pure fiction, is the One China Policy. The One China Policy was formally stated in the Shanghai Communique of 1972, between President Richard Nixon and Premier Zhou Enlai [20]. It states that there is only one China, and that Taiwan is part of China. It is pure fiction because Taiwan and China were then in a state of undeclared war, and neither would concede to be part of the other. Yet because the Nationalists government in Taiwan believed that it represented China, and the PRC government in mainland China also held the same belief, it was a story that met the requirements of the times. The US acknowledged the PRC's position that there is only one China, with Taiwan being a part of it, but did not endorse the PRC's claim of sovereignty over Taiwan. Second, the Shanghai Communique was based on the principle of agreeing to disagree. There were fundamental disagreements that the US and China could not come to accord, so they agreed to state their respective positions, next to each other, believing that agreeing to disagree can be the basis for an honest and sustainable relationship.

Among other diverging positions, the US and China stated their respective views on Vietnam, the Korean peninsula, and on Taiwan. The US "stressed that the peoples of Indochina should be allowed to determine their destiny without outside intervention; its constant primary objective has been a negotiated solution; the eight-point proposal put forward by the Republic of Vietnam and the United States on January 27, 1972 represents a basis for the attainment of that objective." Moreover, "the United States will maintain its close ties with and support for the

Republic of Korea; the United States will support efforts of the Republic of Korea to seek a relaxation of tension and increased communication in the Korean peninsula." A paragraph removed, the Chinese side "expressed its firm support to the peoples of Vietnam, Laos, and Cambodia in their efforts for the attainment of their goal and its firm support to the seven-point proposal of the Provisional Revolutionary Government of the Republic of South Vietnam and the elaboration of February this year on the two key problems in the proposal, and to the Joint Declaration of the Summit Conference of the Indochinese Peoples." In addition, "it firmly supports the eight-point program for the peaceful unification of Korea put forward by the Government of the Democratic People's Republic of Korea on April 12, 1971, and the stand for the abolition of the UN Commission for the Unification and Rehabilitation of Korea." On the issue of Taiwan, the Chinese side reaffirmed its position: "The Taiwan question is the crucial question obstructing the normalization of relations between China and the United States; the Government of the People's Republic of China is the sole legal government of China; Taiwan is a province of China which has long been returned to the motherland; the liberation of Taiwan is China's internal affair in which no other country has the right to interfere; and all US forces and military installations must be withdrawn from Taiwan." The US side declared: "The United States acknowledges that all Chinese on either side of the Taiwan Strait maintain there is but one China and that Taiwan is a part of China. The United States Government does not challenge that position. It reaffirms its interest in a peaceful settlement of the Taiwan question by the Chinese themselves. With this prospect in mind, it affirms the ultimate objective of the withdrawal of all US forces and military installations from Taiwan. In the meantime, it will progressively reduce its forces and military installations on Taiwan as the tension in the area diminishes." Stripped of the dry diplomatic language, the US and China, sworn enemies of the Cold War, laid down their differences side by side, their opposing support for South and North Korea, South and North Vietnam, and their fundamental differences over Taiwan, so that a new chapter in relations may emerge.

In his toasts at the banquet honoring his visit to Beijing in 1972, President Richard Nixon made the following remarks, "let us recognize at the outset these points: We have at times in the past been enemies. We have great differences today. What brings us together is that we have common interests which transcend those differences. As we discuss our differences, neither of us will compromise our principles. But while we cannot close the gulf between us, we can try to bridge it so that we may be able to talk across it... What legacy shall we leave our children? Are they destined to die for the hatreds which have plagued the old world, or are they destined to live because we had the vision to build a new world [21]?" On February 25th, 2022, the Committee of 100, jointly with the American Chamber of Commerce in Shanghai, and the National Committee on United States-China Relations (NCUSCR), hosted a half-day session celebrating the 50th anniversary of the signing of the Shanghai Communiqué, which lay the foundation for 50 years of peace and prosperity in Asia [22]. Henry Kissinger, and Zhou Bingde, niece of Premier Zhou Enlai, who helped broker the Shanghai Communiqué for the Chinese side, delivered prepared remarks. Today, there are sporadic attempts to create new stories that can meet the challenges of the times. A former Vice President of Taiwan, Annette Lu, proposed a Chinese Commonwealth that would be integrated economically, like the European Union, but remain separate politically [23] I have no idea what a modern story would be that could serve the interests of Taiwan, US, and China. I don't even know if any or all of the parties are interested in or have the prerequisite trust to engage in such myth making. But what I do know is that military deterrence gives us precious time, so that visionary leaders on all sides may seek out a better solution, one that doesn't involve devastating economic and human costs on all sides, and one that finds common ground despite the differences.

I spoke to George Yeo, Minister of Foreign Affairs for Singapore between 2004 and 2011. George believes that the people of Asia Pacific want peace, and there needn't be hegemony by any country in the region. The world is moving towards a multipolar configuration, and the US can remain the primus inter pares, or first among equals. More importantly, it could become the coordinating rather than the dominating power. He thinks that the Chinese don't want a war, but are preparing for one, for example by increasing their nuclear arsenal significantly as a second-strike nuclear deterrence. An armed conflict between the US and China would likely draw in other countries, within and outside the region. George held up Matteo Ricci (1552–1610), an Italian Jesuit missionary who introduced Christian teachings to China in the sixteenth century. Ricci lived in China for nearly 30 years and preached that dialog, exchange, and consistency form the basis for mutual understanding [24].

The South China Sea connects the main arteries of trade in Southeast Asia. It also serves as the maritime boundary for the first island chain. To become the dominant power in Asia, China must first become the preeminent power in the first island chain, as it relies heavily on the strategic waterways for maritime trade to secure its economy [25]. Located at the midpoint of the first island chain, Taiwan is about more than Taiwan. The defense of Taiwan is about the defense of American interests in Asia. But what interests is America defending there? I have had the opportunity to travel to almost all Southeast Asian countries. Across those that I have visited, the feedback is consistent. First, there is no desire to see an armed conflict between the US and PRC, and second, there is real desire to see a continued and enhanced role for America in Southeast Asia [26]. The ten countries of Southeast Asia, including Brunei, Myanmar, Cambodia, Indonesia, Laos, Malaysia, the Philippines, Singapore, Thailand and Vietnam, collectively form the Association of Southeast Asian Nations (ASEAN). With a projected regional annual growth rate of about 5%, Southeast Asia is expected to collectively become the fourth largest economy in the world, overtaking the European Union and Japan by 2050. With a median age of around 28 years old, Southeast Asia offers tremendous market opportunities for US companies [27]. ASEAN countries are already the fourth largest export market for the United States after Canada, Mexico, and China. US export growth to Southeast Asia has been steady since the 1997 Asian financial crisis, aside from a dip in 2009, and reached \$86.2 billion in 2018, accounting for 5.2% of overall US exports. ASEAN countries are also the fourth largest source of US imports after Canada, Mexico, and China. Following the 2008 global financial crisis, US imports from Southeast Asia have grown steadily and reached over \$185.8 billion in 2018, up 9.4% from 2017 and up 68.7% in the last decade. Overall, US imports from ASEAN account for 7.3% of US imports.

Yet these numbers are dwarfed by trade between China and Southeast Asia. China has retained its position as ASEAN's largest trading partner since 2009. Trade between ASEAN and China has more than doubled since 2010, from \$235.5 billion to \$507.9 billion in 2019 (18% of ASEAN's total) and almost quadrupled since the entry into force of the ASEAN-China Trade in Goods Agreement in 2005. ASEAN's exports to China grew at an average annual rate of 10.4% from 2010 to 2019, as compared to 12.5% for ASEAN's import from China during the same period. Despite the COVID-19 pandemic, the trade volume between

ASEAN and China increased by 2.2% in the first half of 2020 during which ASEAN leapt to become China's largest trading partner for the first time, making ASEAN and China each other's top trading partner [28].

It is against this economic backdrop that the Obama administration negotiated the Trans-Pacific Partnership (TPP). As a group, the 11 TPP countries are the largest goods and services export market of the United States. US goods exports to TPP countries totaled $698 billion in 2013, representing 44% of total US goods exports. US exports of agricultural products to TPP countries totaled $63 billion in 2013, representing 42% of total US agricultural exports. US private services exports to TPP countries totaled $172 billion in 2012, representing 27% of total US private services exports to the world [29]. However, on the third day of his first presidency, President Trump pulled out of TPP, citing lack of protection for American workers. Without the US, a modified Comprehensive and Progressive Agreement for Trans-Pacific Partnership (CPTPP), or TPP-11, was signed by 11 Asia Pacific economies on March 2018 that entered into force on December 2018. CPTPP is the largest Free Trade Agreement in Asia Pacific, with a market of 490 million people, covering 12.9% of the world's gross domestic product and 14.9% of global trade volume. According to OECD calculations, the CPTPP procurement market is a $1.9 trillion opportunity for its members [27].

Under the Biden Administration, the US launched the Indo-Pacific Economic Framework for Prosperity (IPEF) with 13 countries including Australia, Brunei, Fiji, India, Indonesia, Japan, South Korea, Malaysia, New Zealand, Philippines, Singapore, Thailand, and Vietnam. The Framework is predicated on the following four pillars: (1) Trade, (2) Supply Chains, (3) Clean Energy, Decarbonization, and Infrastructure, and (4) Tax and Anti-Corruption. The IPEF is designed to be flexible, meaning that IPEF partners do not need to join all four pillars [30]. Unlike a traditional trade agreement, there is no promise of greater US market access, and a lack of enforcement mechanisms limits the ability of the US to secure long-term compliance. Then on April 2, 2025, President Trump announced Liberation Day, imposing an expansive new slate of tariffs on about sixty countries or trading blocs that held trade deficit with the US. The goal is to secure a bilateral trade agreement with each country or trading bloc, or absent such an agreement, to impose unilateral tariffs set by the US [31]. Experts note that today, it is near impossible to get a multilateral trade agreement passed in Congress. Yet without deepening trade and economic relationships with Southeast Asia, American military and security guarantees alone simply won't suffice.

The better assumption should be for America to enhance and integrate our economic interests in Asia. As much as this is a foreign policy decision, it is also a domestic policy choice, with the need to convince American voters why deepened economic integration with Asia is in America's interest. This assumption will necessarily lead to a more strategic, more multi-pronged, and more durable approach than simply trying everything to the military defense of Taiwan. American assumptions in Asia should not solely depend on whether the US comes to Taiwan's military aid, or the outcome of an armed conflict between the US and PRC. America has an obligation to all its allies, including Taiwan, but American interests in Asia is much broader and deeper than Taiwan. By focusing on enhancing and integrating American economic interests throughout Asia, we will likely strengthen our defense of Taiwan.

Military deterrence will buy us time. Perhaps 2 years, perhaps 5 years, perhaps 10 years, perhaps longer. This is precious time that we can use to seek out a better solution to war. Due to pandemic lockdowns and the worsening in relations, American and Chinese leaders have not spoken much to each other in person. Instead, we have witnessed a war of words across cyberspace, in which missteps easily morph into crises. In January 2023, a Chinese ballon crossed into US airspace. American officials claimed that it was a spy ballon conducting espionage. The resulting controversy raised significant hostilities towards China, with Secretary of State Anthony Blinken canceling a previously scheduled diplomatic trip to China. The balloon was shot down. In the days after its wreckage was recovered, US officials declared that the balloon was "clearly for intelligence surveillance [32]." But after months of analysis, officials quietly walked back those claims. Seven months later, Chairman of Joint Chief of Staff Milley told "CBS News Sunday Morning" that the balloon wasn't spying: "The intelligence community, their assessment—and it's a high-confidence assessment—[is] that there was no intelligence collection by that balloon [33]." In November 2023, President Biden and President Xi met in person for several hours on the sidelines of the Asia–Pacific Economic Cooperation (APEC) Summit in San Francisco, after zero direct contacts between the two leaders for almost a year. President Biden characterized the talks as the "most constructive and productive" since he came to office [34]. On June 5, 2025, President Trump spoke to President Xi for 90 minutes that led to a pause in trade disputes [35]. American, Chinese, or people of any nationality, we are all humans. Humans do best when we discuss our differences in person, face to face, over time, and in private. So much trust has been lost during the past years, and even worse, so little interactions have occurred that have led to any meaningful dialog. Some experts I have spoken to are skeptical that it is worthwhile talking to the PRC about peace in the Asia Pacific [36]. Some experts I have spoken to are skeptical that the US political environment would allow any divergence from our current assumptions towards the PRC in the Asia Pacific. Perhaps they are correct. But the alternatives seem much worse.

References

1. U.S. Department of Defense (2023) Military and security developments involving the People's Republic of China. Available at: https://media.defense.gov/2023/Oct/19/2003323409/-1/-1/1/2023-MILITARY-AND-SECURITY-DEVELOPMENTS-INVOLVING-THE-PEOPLES-REPUBLIC-OF-CHINA.PDF. Accessed 14 Aug 2025.
2. U.S. Department of Defense (2023) U.S. focuses on deterrence as China raises stakes in Indo-Pacific. Available at: https://www.defense.gov/News/News-Stories/Article/Article/3566970/us-focuses-on-deterrence-as-china-raises-stakes-in-indo-pacific/. Accessed 14 Aug 2025.
3. U.S. Department of Defense (2023) DOD report details Chinese efforts to build military power. Available at: https://www.defense.gov/News/News-Stories/Article/Article/3562442/dod-report-details-chinese-efforts-to-build-military-power/. Accessed 14 Aug 2025.
4. U.S. Department of Defense (2023) Opening Testimony by Secretary of Defense Lloyd J. Austin III Before the House Appropriations Committee Budget Posture Hearing. Available at: https://www.defense.gov/News/Speeches/Speech/Article/3338649/opening-testimony-by-secretary-of-defense-lloyd-j-austin-iii-before-the-house-a/. Accessed 14 Aug 2025.
5. U.S. Department of State (n.d.) Roosevelt Corollary to the Monroe Doctrine, 1904. Available at: https://history.state.gov/milestones/1899-1913/roosevelt-and-monroe-doctrine. Accessed 14 Aug 2025.
6. PBS NewsHour (2021) Watch: Gen. Milley explains his calls with China over concerns about President Trump. Available at: https://www.pbs.org/newshour/politics/watch-gen-milley-explains-his-calls-with-china-over-concerns-about-president-trump. Accessed 14 Aug 2025.

7. The Guardian (2023) US general's 'gut feeling' of war with China sparks alarm over predictions. Available at: https://www.theguardian.com/world/2023/feb/02/us-general-gut-feeling-war-china-sparks-alarm-predictions. Accessed 14 Aug 2025.
8. Government of Taiwan (n.d.) History of Taiwan. Available at: https://www.taiwan.gov.tw/content_3.php. Accessed 14 Aug 2025.
9. U.S. Department of State (n.d.) Taiwan Strait crises: 1954–1955 and 1958. Available at: https://history.state.gov/milestones/1953-1960/taiwan-strait-crises. Accessed 14 Aug 2025.
10. CNBC (2022) Taiwan's trade with China is far bigger than its trade with the U.S. Available at: https://www.cnbc.com/2022/08/05/taiwans-trade-with-china-is-far-bigger-than-its-trade-with-the-us.html. Accessed 14 Aug 2025.
11. Government of Taiwan (n.d.) Cross-Strait Relations. Available at: https://www.taiwan.gov.tw/content_6.php. Accessed 14 Aug 2025.
12. Worldcrunch (2023) The Taiwan Paradox: Preparing For War And Ready To Do Business With China. Available at: https://worldcrunch.com/world-affairs/taiwan-ukraine-china. Accessed 14 Aug 2025.
13. CNN (2023) Beijing warns of 'severe impact' on US–China relations as Taiwan's leader lands in New York. Available at: https://www.cnn.com/2023/03/30/asia/tsai-ing-wen-taiwan-new-york-city-china-response-intl-hnk/index.html. Accessed 14 Aug 2025.
14. U.S. Department of State (2020) Addressing China's Military Aggression in the Indo-Pacific Region. Available at: https://2017-2021.state.gov/chinas-military-aggression-in-the-indo-pacific-region/. Accessed 14 Aug 2025.
15. Taipei Times (2023) Poll shows 48.9% support independence. Available at: https://www.taipeitimes.com/News/taiwan/archives/2023/09/02/2003805648. Accessed 14 Aug 2025.
16. U.S. Congress (1979) Taiwan Relations Act. Available at: https://www.congress.gov/bill/96th-congress/house-bill/2479/all-info. Accessed 14 Aug 2025.
17. Council on Foreign Relations (n.d.) Strategic ambiguity toward Taiwan. Available at: https://modeldiplomacy.cfr.org/pop-up-cases/strategic-ambiguity-toward-taiwan. Accessed 14 Aug 2025.
18. Center for Strategic and International Studies (2023) The first battle of the next war: Wargaming a Chinese invasion of Taiwan. Available at: https://www.csis.org/analysis/first-battle-next-war-wargaming-chinese-invasion-taiwan. Accessed 14 Aug 2025.
19. Council on Foreign Relations (2023) Why is important to the United States. Available at: https://www.cfr.org/blog/why-taiwan-important-united-states. Accessed 14 Aug 2025.

20. U.S. Department of State (1972) Joint Statement Following Discussions With Leaders of the People's Republic of China. Available at: https://history.state.gov/historicaldocuments/frus1969-76v17/d203. Accessed 14 Aug 2025.
21. University of California Santa Barbara (1972) Toasts of the President and Premier Chou En-lai at the People's Republic of China banquet honoring President Nixon. Available at: https://www.presidency.ucsb.edu/documents/toasts-the-president-and-premier-chou-en-lai-the-peoples-republic-china-banquet-honoring. Accessed 14 Aug 2025.
22. Committee of 100 (2022) Shanghai Communiqué 50th anniversary commemoration. Available at: https://www.committee100.org/events/shanghai-communique-50th-anniversary-commemoration/. Accessed 14 Aug 2025.
23. New York Times (2023) A Chinese Commonwealth? An Unpopular Idea Resurfaces in Taiwan. Available at: https://www.nytimes.com/2023/03/12/opinion/international-world/taiwan-china.html. Accessed 14 Aug 2025.
24. America Magazine (2023) Pope Francis: Jesuit Matteo Ricci brought the Catholic faith to China with dialogue, friendship and consistency. Available at: https://www.americamagazine.org/faith/2023/05/31/francis-general-audience-matteo-ricci-evangelization-245390. Accessed 14 Aug 2025.
25. Australian Institute of International Affairs (2020) The Taiwan Frontier and the Chinese Dominance for the Second Island Chain. Available at: https://www.internationalaffairs.org.au/australianoutlook/taiwan-frontier-chinese-dominance-for-second-island-chain/. Accessed 14 Aug 2025.
26. McKinsey & Company (2022) The Asian century, two years on: A look back. Available at: https://www.mckinsey.com/featured-insights/future-of-asia/the-asian-century-two-years-on-a-look-back. Accessed 14 Aug 2025.
27. Center for Strategic and International Studies (2019) U.S.–Southeast Asia trade relations in an age of disruption. Available at: https://www.csis.org/analysis/us-southeast-asia-trade-relations-age-disruption. Accessed 14 Aug 2025.
28. Association of Southeast Asian Nations (n.d.) ASEAN–China economic relations. Available at: https://asean.org/our-communities/economic-community/integration-with-global-economy/asean-china-economic-relation/. Accessed 14 Aug 2025.
29. Office of the United States Trade Representative (n.d.) Overview of the TPP. Available at: https://ustr.gov/tpp/overview-of-the-TPP. Accessed 14 Aug 2025.

30. Office of the United States Trade Representative (n.d.) Indo-Pacific Economic Framework for Prosperity (IPEF). Available at: https://ustr.gov/trade-agreements/agreements-under-negotiation/indo-pacific-economic-framework-prosperity-ipef. Accessed 14 Aug 2025.
31. Council on Foreign Relations (2025) What Trump Trade Policy Has Achieved Since 'Liberation Day'. Available at: https://www.cfr.org/article/what-trump-trade-policy-has-achieved-liberation-day. Accessed 14 Aug 2025.
32. CNN (2023) US officials disclosed new details about the balloon's capabilities. Here's what we know. Available at: https://www.cnn.com/2023/02/09/politics/spy-balloon-technology/index.html. Accessed 14 Aug 2025.
33. CBS News (2023) The bizarre secret behind China's spy balloon. Available at: https://www.cbsnews.com/news/the-bizarre-secret-behind-chinas-spy-balloon/. Accessed 14 Aug 2025.
34. The White House (2023) Remarks by President Biden in a press conference, Woodside, CA. Available at: https://bidenwhitehouse.archives.gov/briefing-room/speeches-remarks/2023/11/16/remarks-by-president-biden-in-a-press-conference-woodside-ca/. Accessed 14 Aug 2025.
35. CBS News (2025) Trump speaks to Xi on trade, says talks between U.S. and China will resume soon. Available at: https://www.cbsnews.com/news/trump-xi-jinping-trade-tariffs-phone-call/. Accessed 14 Aug 2025.
36. Wall Street Journal (2023) Zombie engagement with Beijing. Available at: https://www.wsj.com/articles/zombie-engagement-with-beijing-biden-xi-spy-cuba-tech-human-rights-b79bc890. Accessed 14 Aug 2025.

CHAPTER 8

The Road Ahead

The US–China relationship may ultimately be defined and remembered by hard power, but it is shaped by choices. How should America respond? What assumptions should guide our choices? What may we expect from the Chinese in any response? And what role can ordinary citizens play in shaping a more just and secure future for all parties? This book began with an examination of the Vietnam War and the Cold War because history offers lessons. We would be wise to remember what happens when assumptions go unchallenged and a conflict that no ordinary American wants consumes generations. Then, as now, policymakers insist on strength rather than diplomacy, assumptions harden into absolutes, and each small step leads inevitably to the next irreversible step. Yet we can avoid another Vietnam War. We can resist another Cold War. China is a measurable threat, but the larger threat is how we respond, driven by fear or guided by facts and values.

In this book I have tried to stay away from the Chinese perspective. For example, most historians of China agree that the Chinese had suffered a century of humiliation at the hands of foreign powers from the mid-nineteenth to the mid-twentieth century, and that this is one of the

Z. Z. Huang, *Rethinking China*,
https://doi.org/10.1007/978-981-95-3608-5_8

driving forces for the national rejuvenation that President Xi frequently quotes [1]. I don't discuss them because as valid as these perspectives may be in the eyes of the Chinese, and as useful as they maybe in a context of exchange with the Chinese, they do not impact how Americans measure our values and interests. Similarly, in my conversations with experts, a good number of them have brought up instances in which the US has fallen short on our own stated positions. For instance, while the US criticizes the PRC for violating the rulings of an international tribunal on the South China Sea, it itself has not ratified the United Nations Convention on the Law of the Sea, under which the rulings derive credence [2]. While the US criticizes China for stymying inquiries into the treatment of Uyghurs in Xinjiang, it has itself not demonstrated accountability in Iraq and obstructed investigations of war crimes committed there [3]. I believe that America should always strive to live up to our values, but we have the right, as any nation does, to speak up when universal values are under assault or our national interests are undermined. There are many issues that divide the US and PRC that are not covered in this book. For example, it is not an assumption but a fact that American companies do not face a level playing field in China. Or a fact that the PRC is seeking to reshape the global information environment in its interests [4]. Though these issues are important, I chose to focus instead on the assumptions that have fueled the hysteria over China, and underpin the argument for an existential struggle with the PRC.

The thrust of this book is not whether China is a threat to the US. The purpose of this book, as stated in the introduction, is to use all available data and evidence to help illustrate what threat level is China. This is of the utmost importance because depending on the threat level, we respond accordingly and appropriately. As the data and evidence clearly illustrate, because of the hysteria over China, we have already committed actions that have hurt our values and competitiveness. Because of the hysteria, we have missed the forest for the trees in important areas. Most worrisome is the fact that under the current set of assumptions, we may be sleepwalking into an armed conflict that will put American lives, treasures, and our comprehensive interests in Asia in jeopardy. I have asked thoughtful experts whom I have become familiar with why this is so. They have generally offered fear as an explanation. It is understandable to fear the loss of our economic pre-eminence in the world. It is also understandable to fear that what we believed to be true all along—that the American model is the best model in the world, that the American way of life is the most aspired to in the world—may not be entirely true. The other driver of fear towards China is more insidious. It harkens back to the century old trope of the Yellow Peril, the belief that Asians, in particular the Chinese, are inherently foreign and alien and bent on the destruction and subjugation of the Western world.

Recent statements by American leaders have ranged from "But when you see China, these are fierce people in terms of negotiation. They want to take your throat out, they want to cut you apart. These are tough people. I've dealt with them all my life," to "The Chinese government purposefully hid the disease, even from its own people, so they could send it around the world. That's how little regard they have for human life," to "Imperialist, authoritarian China will do anything it can to bend the global economy to its own will and make the world adopt their Communist way of life [5]." Alas, fear sells. Especially at the ballot box. Fear can easily turn into anger. Anger that our seemingly intractable domestic problems, whether they be regional or racial economic disparities, substance abuse or drug epidemics, disinformation or erosion in trust in public institutions, are attributable solely to a foreign actor. And nothing motivates a person to get up and vote more than fear and anger. This is why China has become a prime target in election seasons [6].

In 2012, President Obama countered Republican challenger Mitt Romney's criticism of his China policies by capitalizing on a New York Times exposé of Romney's China linked business interests. In 2016, Donald Trump made China a centerpiece of his election campaign, decrying the PRC government's systematic harm to the US through unfair trade practices, currency manipulation, and IP theft. In 2019, President Trump called for investigations of Hunter Biden, Joe Biden's son, for his dealings with a Chinese private equity firm. China has even crept into local and state elections. During the 2022 midterm election cycle, in the Pennsylvania GOP Senate primary race, TV personality Mehmet Oz ("Dr. Oz") and hedge fund manager David McCormick made each other's China-related business investments a key campaign platform. "Beijing's favorite candidate, David McCormick, has outsourced American jobs and he's made millions investing in China in partnership with the CCP," said Oz's Communications Director Brittany Yanick in a statement. McCormick's campaign retaliated by noting that "The Dr. Oz Show" had a lucrative product promotional agreement with Usana Health Sciences, a company whose largest single market is China. A similar mud fight unfolded in the GOP Senate primary in Missouri between Missouri

Attorney General Eric Schmitt and former Governor Eric Greitens. A Greitens PAC video called out Schmitt for his support in 2011 of the St. Louis International Airport's Aerotropolis or "China Hub," designed to make the city the axis of air cargo between China and the Midwest. The ad's kicker: "Eric Schmitt: Good for China. Bad for Missouri." A Schmitt PAC video retaliated by slamming Greitens for an appearance on Chinese state television during an official visit to Beijing while governor in 2017. The ad's kicker: "Eric Greitens: Good for China. Bad for Missouri [6]."

In a 2021 Gallup poll, 45% of Americans viewed China as America's greatest enemy, more than double the percentage who said so in 2020. A new high of 63% of Americans saw China's economic power as a critical threat to the vital interests of the US in the next 10 years [7]. America has been here before. In the 1980s, experts were predicting that Japan may soon overtake the US to become the world's largest economy. "Japan's trade practices are not just unfair; they're predatory. They're aimed at dominating industries and destroying competitors," cried Donald Trump, businessman and future US president. "Japanese industrial policy has become a competitive threat to our economic well-being," declared Michael Dukakis, former Governor of Massachusetts and Democratic Presidential nominee in 1988. "The rise of Japanese pop culture is a threat to the moral fabric of our society," pronounced Tipper Gore, former Second Lady of the US. In 1982, Vincent Chin, a Chinese American, was beaten to death by two auto workers in Detroit, Michigan who mistook Chin for Japanese and blamed him for the mass layoffs then occurring in the auto industry [8]. Yet unbounded by fear, Americans also got curious. American entrepreneurs started learning from the Japanese. When I studied Industrial Engineering at Stanford University in the 1990s, I learned about Six Sigma, a set of management techniques that greatly reduces the probability of error or defect by improving business processes. American companies, from General Electric to Ford Motor Company, adopted Six Sigma and the Japanese philosophy of Kaizen, or continuous improvement. Through Stanford's overseas program, I studied in Japan and then worked at Hitachi Ltd in Tokyo, learning firsthand the merits of Japanese manufacturing and industrial processes.

Today, in a reversal of industry convention, many global carmakers are looking to learn from their Chinese rivals. Ford CEO Jim Farley, speaking at the Aspen Idea Summit, called his trips visiting Chinese vehicle manufacturers the most humbling thing he'd ever seen. "And even beyond that, their cost, their quality of their vehicles is far superior to what I see in the West," Farley continued. "We are in a global competition with China, and it's not just EVs. And if we lose this we do not have a future at Ford." So, what's Ford doing to manage the situation? It's learning from China. Farley said he brings his entire leadership team on his trips to the country, where they drive as many of the latest cars that they can. "Then we pick the four or five that we love and then we put them on a plane and fly them to Detroit. And then we drive the crap out of them, and then we take them apart and we put them back together," he said. Ford is also working on a $30,000 electric car that Farley called "the Model T of EVs." It's building up manufacturing of cheaper lithium iron phosphate, or LFP, batteries in Michigan through a licensing agreement with China's CATL. Due to the hysteria over China, that partnership has been mired in political controversy, but Ford argued it's necessary to build affordable EVs in America. "People don't realize that China has IP that America needs," he said. "I think we just need to be more humble as a country that they do things really well, that we need to learn [9]." "Despite slower EV industry growth, we believe the long-term future is profitable electric vehicle production," said GM CEO Mary T. Barra, as the company plans to import EV batteries from China's CATL despite steep tariffs [10, 11]. Volkswagen and Nissan are adopting some Chinese ways to be speedier as well [12].

Interestingly, many US–China experts are Jewish Americans. As I have gotten to know them well, we often discuss similarities between the Jewish and Chinese traditions: the love of family, the deference for education, and the respect for hard work. Values that resonant strongly with American values. We also found a mutual curiosity in how the Jewish and Chinese civilizations have survived for more than four thousand years and are now re-emerging as significant players on the global stage. Great civilizations have abounded throughout human history. Some like the Babylonians or Assyrians, no longer exist. Some like the Egyptians and Persians, are largely disconnected from their ancient pasts. While still others, like the Greeks and Italians, built great empires but are now a shadow of their former selves. Civilizations that have withstood the ravages of time—like the Indian, Chinese, Jewish, etc.—that have kept their traditions yet marched with modernity, should beg our curiosity rather than fear. For America is best at integrating the world's best ideas and talents, and then making them uniquely our own. We are not only a land of immigrants; we are a land of immigrant ideas. We rise to the occasion each time because of our ability to adapt and learn and innovate. For example, the origin of American design was heavily dependent on contemporary modernist design movements in France, Germany, and Scandinavia. After World War II, America brought thousands of German scientists, engineers, and technicians to the US for rocket development and eventually spaceflight. Just like French design or German engineering, we today make what is Chinese uniquely American. With more than 45,000 Chinese restaurants in the US, if there is a national cuisine for America, it may just be Chinese [13]. But as anyone who has been to China will attest, Chinese food in the US tastes different from Chinese food in China. In the US, we have created American Chinese food, just as we have done with Italian pizza and German hamburgers. I am often reminded of the fact that at 249 years old, America is younger than most dynasties in Chinese history. The last imperial dynasty, the Qing dynasty, lasted 267 years. If we are to continue our trajectory of growth, we must never turn inward, and continue to learn from the best of what the world has to offer, including from China, past and present.

Yet I am notably worried. Because of the hysteria over China many American students have lost interest in studying Chinese and spending time in China. Political candidates attack each other for having any dealings or interactions with China. The feeling in Washington D.C. is that the less time you have spent in China, in business or cultural dealings, the safer you are politically. I have had a chance to speak with many of the directors of Chinese Flagship Programs across American universities. The Language Flagship Program is a program sponsored by the National Security Education Program (NSEP) and the US Department of Defense. The goal of the Language Flagship Program is to create language capable professionals in various fields of study to enhance US competitiveness and security [14]. These programs are critical because if we are to deal effectively with a resurgent China, or for that matter any country, we need Americans who speak the language, understand the culture, and have significant experiences working with the country. The feedback from many directors of Chinese Flagship Programs is that interest from students have declined dramatically. Many don't see a good career path to studying Chinese. Many cite the deterioration in relations between the US and China as a significant deterrent. In 2009, President Obama launched the "100,000 Strong" initiative to encourage 100,000 American students to study in China [15]. Fast forward to 2022, there were 350 American students studying in China versus 300,000 Chinese students studying in the US [16]. Even more troubling, the Fulbright scholarships, which since 1979 have provided Americans with the opportunity to study, teach, and conduct research in China and have trained generations of American leaders versed in China, was suspended by President Trump in 2020. It has yet to be re-enacted even though everyone I have spoken to points to its one-sided benefit to America [17]. A proposed bill—H.R.8939 (Restoring Fulbright Exchanges with China and Hong Kong Act)—is stuck in Congress [18]. In 2019, there were more than 300 flights per week between the US and China, but as of November 2023, the number is estimated to be about 70 flights per week. More and more, friends approach me about the safety of traveling to China for sightseeing, often citing vague fears of unlawful detainment.

The 2024 presidential election is behind us. Presidential candidates from both political parties tried to outdo each other by acting tough on China. Yet I believe that a rising America is not incompatible with a resurgent China. And America First is compatible with America Leads. Imagine a presidential candidate who argues the following:

- China is a worthy competitor. Chinese companies are innovative. Chinese workers are hardworking. And the Chinese government takes all measures to ensure its own success.
- The US will outcompete China, and for that matter, any country, by doing what we do best. By investing in our people, our infrastructure, and the jobs of tomorrow. And by being the most attractive place on the planet for talent and capital from around the globe.
- The US will invest strategically in regions hardest hit by globalization, and thoughtfully with taxpayer dollars on any industrial policy.
- The US will not give in to the rhetoric of fear and anger. We will ensure that our values are protected at home, in particular for Chinese and Asian Americans.
- The US will work with our friends and allies, and through leading and strengthening international rules-based systems, take China to task whenever it violates its commitments to the international community, be they on trade, human rights, intellectual property, etc.
- The US will deepen our economic engagement in the Asia Pacific. We will strengthen our military capabilities in the region because it affords us an opportunity to explore a future of peace and prosperity

that has a role for all interested parties, including the US, China, and in particular Taiwan.
- The US will collaborate with China on matters of shared interest, including climate change, nuclear nonproliferation, preventing the next pandemic, and developing the Global South.

These are worthwhile arguments to be made by any presidential candidate. Yet that presidential candidate may be attacked for being naive on China. For not recognizing that China is an existential threat to America. For not recognizing that China is trying to infiltrate the US, hoist its authoritarian system upon the world, cheat and steal from American workers, forcibly take over Taiwan, and destroy the international rules-based system that the US has fought so hard to create. That presidential candidate may calmly reply that the data and evidence underlying the hysteria over China are highly suspect. On the other hand, we have already seen clear data and evidence that the hysteria over China is hurting American values and competitiveness. Yet even if elements of the hysteria were true, that China poses measurable threat to America, the arguments made by our imaginary presidential candidate are still the best courses of action to surmount the likely threats and challenges. These courses of action are not only effective in dealing with China, but serve an even more important purpose. They ensure that we do not externalize our domestic problems.

It is easy to externalize our domestic problems. And many politicians do this precisely because it is easy. As David Halberstam had observed after the Vietnam War, "it was one of the great myths of that time that foreign policy was this pure and uncontaminated area which was never touched by domestic politics, and that domestic politics ended at the water's edge. The truth, in sharp contrast, was that all those critical decisions were primarily driven by considerations of domestic politics, and by political fears of the consequences of looking weak in a forthcoming domestic election... One had to stop totalitarianism, and since the only thing the totalitarians understood was force, one had to be willing to use force. They justified each decision to use power by their own conviction that the Communists were worse, which justified our dirty tricks, our toughness [19]." Yet even if we took down China, the jobs of yesterday will still not come back to the heartland of America. Even if we took down China, economic and geographic disparities will still remain in America. Even if we took down China, racial and social wounds will still haunt

America. Only by focusing clearheadedly and wholeheartedly on our own domestic problems can we hope to solve them. Otherwise, even if we manage to take down China, there will be other fierce global competitors such as India waiting in the near horizon. After Harvard Business School, I spent a summer working for Infosys, India's second largest IT company, in Bangalore, India. Inspired by the dynamism and drive that I had witnessed, I later set up a development center in Gurgaon, India for the financial services data company. India has its own set of unique challenges, but with the largest youth population in the world, with a hunger for progress and growth, it is set to create jobs for and take jobs away from the rest of the world. Any student of history will note that great empires most often fall not because of the ascendancy of a foreign rival, but rather from internal decay and dissent, and unnecessary and excessive war making.

I do not suppose such a presidential candidate will emerge in any immediate presidential election. I do not presume that any politician will openly challenge the prevalent assumptions about China. But I take solace in knowing that more than sixty years ago, at the height of the Cold War, President John F. Kennedy made an unprecedented Commencement Address at American University in Washington D.C., that changed how we engaged with the Soviet Union [20]. Just 9 months prior, the US and Soviet Union had come perilously close to nuclear war during the Cuban Missile Crisis. In the aftermath of the Crisis, President Kennedy realized that a new course must be taken to avert a global catastrophe. In his address, he declared: "let us not be blind to our differences—but let us also direct attention to our common interests and to the means by which those differences can be resolved. And if we cannot end now our differences, at least we can help make the world safe for diversity… We are not here distributing blame or pointing the finger of judgment. We must deal with the world as it is, and not as it might have been had the history of the last 18 years been different… For we can seek a relaxation of tension without relaxing our guard. And, for our part, we do not need to use threats to prove that we are resolute. We do not need to jam foreign broadcasts out of fear our faith will be eroded. We are unwilling to impose our system on any unwilling people—but we are willing and able to engage in peaceful competition with any people on earth. Meanwhile, we seek to strengthen the United Nations, to help solve its financial problems, to make it a more effective instrument for peace, to develop it into a genuine world security system—a system capable of resolving disputes on the basis of law, of insuring the security of the large and the small, and of creating conditions under which nuclear arms can finally be abolished… Finally, my fellow Americans, let us examine our attitude toward peace and freedom here at home. The quality and spirit of our own society must justify and support our efforts abroad… We do not want a war. We do not now expect a war. This generation of Americans has already had enough—more than enough—of war and hate and oppression. We shall be prepared if others wish it. We shall be alert to try to stop it. But we shall also do our part to build a world of peace where the weak are safe and the strong are just." As a result of the speech, less than 2 months later, the Partial Nuclear Test Ban Treaty was signed between the US, USSR, and UK, and a hotline was agreed to between Washington and Moscow.

In this book I have detailed, as much as I can gather, credible ways in which the PRC, intentionally or inadvertently, has hurt the interests of the US and her allies. It is instinctual for humans to want to fight back when faced with a threat or challenge. How do we fight back against transgressions by the PRC? The reality is that the majority of literature out today is on how to be tough on China. Congress has been and continues to pass legislation that punishes perceived transgressions by the PRC. The White House continues to issue regulations that restrict investments, collaborations, and exchanges between the US and PRC. Tried as I might, I could not find any data or evidence to buttress the claims that trade restrictions will bring manufacturing jobs back to America or economic sanctions will improve the lots of oppressed minorities in China. However, I found clear and pressing data and evidence that racial profiling of Chinese American scientists, cessation of US–China scientific collaborations, withdrawal of American leadership from international rules-based systems, military buildup without clear outcomes, hurt American values and interests. In the midst of the hysteria over China, this book aims to explore the underlying assumptions that may better guide our courses of action.

All the proposed assumptions and corresponding courses of action in this book do not require the active participation of the PRC, except in the search for peace in Asia Pacific. On this I have heard many politicians and experts in Washington D.C. say that the Chinese Communist Party cannot be trusted. It is pure evil. And given the CCP's long history of broken promises, oppressions at home and aggressions abroad, the US simply cannot trust anything that the CCP says or agrees to. In addition, many speak to an intention to do ill, to dominate the world, to drive the US out of Asia Pacific, to steal and cheat, that permeates CPP actions. In my dialog with Colin Powell, he had described China as the key strategic challenge for the US, and how much of our responses will be predicated on what we believe to be China's intentions. In our daily dealings, we know by personal experience that depending on our assessment of someone's intentions, we interpret their actions kindly or harshly, with understanding or prejudice. Yet assessing someone's intentions is exceedingly difficult. President Trump has been in the public eye for decades, yet even today Americans disagree vehemently over his intentions, whether as an authoritarian in disguise or a champion for the people. As I have stated at the beginning of this book, I cannot speak to the intentions of President Xi and nor can anyone else. In the book "Difficult Conversations," written by members of the Harvard Negotiation Project, the authors dissected the problem of intention: "The error we make in the realm of intentions is simple but profound: we assume we know the intentions of others when we don't. Worse still, when we are unsure about someone's intentions, we too often decide they are bad. The truth is, Intentions are invisible. We assume them from other people's behavior. In other words, we make them up, we invent them. But our invented stories about other people's intentions are accurate much less often than we think. Why? Because people's intentions, like so much else in difficult conversations, are complex. Sometimes people act with mixed intentions. Sometimes they act with no intentions, or at least not related to us. And sometimes they act on good intentions that nonetheless hurt us." That is why the proposed assumptions and courses of action in this book allow us to accommodate any intentions, good or ill, by a friendly or hostile China.

Yet history does provide clues. In my travels in China, I have met many CCP members. It is hard not to given that there are 98 million CCP members in China and most government officials are CCP members. Usually after a dinner packed with local delicacies and liquors, I would ask them to explain to me what socialism with Chinese characteristics means, and what Communism means in a modern Capitalist, market driven economy. I do not suppose the answers that I have gotten represent the thinking of the CCP in general or of President Xi in particular. But more often than not, I am referred to the history of the CCP [21]. The CCP was established by a group of Chinese intellectuals and students in 1921. In the beginning, it had abided by the dictates of its Soviet advisors and attempted to organize Chinese workers to incite worker led rebellions in the cities. When that failed it shifted tactics and instead went into the countryside and focused on organizing the much larger Chinese peasantry. It was so successful in winning peasant support that in 1931, a Chinese Soviet Republic, with a population of 10 million, was setup in southern China. When direct military confrontation with the Nationalists failed, it was forced to abandon its territories, retreat on the Long March, and shift to guerilla warfare. In 1936, the CPP maneuvered a United Front with the Nationalists to fight against Japanese aggressions. It greatly expanded its strength fighting the Japanese and by the end of World War II, controlled areas of some 100 million people. After defeating the Nationalists in a Civil War and establishing the PRC in 1949, the CCP tried to remake Chinese society. In the process, it enacted disastrous policies such as the Great Leap Forward and the Cultural Revolution. The Great Leap Forward led to the death of an estimated 20 million people of starvation between 1959 and 1962. The Cultural Revolution brought along a decade of chaos during which schools closed, factories shuttered, and development stagnated. In 1978, after the death of Chairman Mao, the CCP shifted to usher in the opening up and reform programs, welcoming foreign capital and expertise [22]. Recently, after 3 years of pandemic lockdowns and strict quarantines, the CCP quickly shifted to full and unrestricted opening in the beginning of 2023 after spontaneous protests spread across the country [23]. Throughout its hundred plus years of party history, the CCP has proven flexible and adaptive, in order to maintain power and control. I don't know if the CCP is trustworthy, but history strongly suggests that it will do what it takes to stay in power. Rational actors, acting on their own interests, offer the foundation for negotiations.

As most of the readers of this book will not be in politics, they are right to ask, what can ordinary American do? A lot. Especially during times when governments don't talk to each other, or talk past each other, people-to-people exchanges and communications are more important than ever. In fact, that's how the US and China started talking to each other more than fifty years ago. The US table tennis team was at the 1971 World Table Tennis Championship in Nagoya, Japan, when American Glenn Cowan missed his team bus following practice and had to board the Chinese team bus. Zhuang Zedong of the Chinese team approached the American, shook his hand, and offered him a depiction of the Huangshan Mountains on a piece of silk cloth. Two days later, the US team received an official invitation to travel to China and play exhibition matches against the Chinese team. The US accepted the invitation and thus begun "Ping Pong diplomacy [24]."

Terry Lautz is the author of "Americans in China," a book that chronicles the lives of ten Americans and their encounters and interactions with the PRC. I have had the pleasure of meeting a good number of the Americans on his list. Couple of the Americans, Shirley Young with General Motors, and Stapleton Roy with the State Department, have already been featured in this book. John Kamm is an American businessman and human rights advocate who has been active in China since 1972. John has made more than 100 trips to China to engage the PRC government on human rights, focusing on prison conditions and the release of political prisoners. In 2004, John received a MacArthur Fellowship for "designing and implementing an original approach to freeing prisoners of conscience in China." To date, he is responsible for the release of hundreds of political prisoners in China. When I spoke with him, he described his ongoing work to improve juvenile justice in China. He also underscored the case of Hong Kong publisher Yao Wentian, who was released from Dongguan Prison in Guangdong province in 2023 due to his efforts. John is sanguine about attacks on him for dealing directly with the PRC government, but stressed that ultimately results matter. In the words of The New York Times, "No other person or organization in the world, including the State Department, has helped more Chinese prisoners [25]."

On a humid New York summer afternoon, I visited Jerome and Joan Cohen at their Park Avenue apartment in Manhattan. Bursting with memorabilia and artworks from China, the apartment is a testament to Jerome and Joan's long-time fascination with law, culture, and the arts in China. As Director of East Asian Legal Studies at Harvard Law School from 1964 to 1979, Jerome helped pioneer the introduction of East Asian legal systems and perspectives into American legal curricula. He also played an important role in helping the Chinese create a whole set of laws that laid the foundation for economic reforms. Joan, on the other hand, made it her mission to promote contemporary Chinese art in the US and to introduce Chinese artists to the West. While much media attention has focused on the politicization of legal proceedings in China, Jerome spoke proudly of his work in helping the Chinese create commercial laws that paved the way for cross-border collaborations and investments.

I asked Terry Lautz how ordinary Americans can benefit from and contribute to people-to-people exchanges between the US and China. Terry replied that given the interwoven dynamics between the US and China, it is ordinary Americans from all walks of life that drive the relationship forward, even though we only hear of household names like Henry Kissinger or Elon Musk. Moreover, American institutions that we don't typically associate with US–China relations can play an important role. He recounted the story of the Philadelphia Orchestra. In 1973, the Philadelphia Orchestra became the first American orchestra to perform in China since 1949. It kicked off "music diplomacy." Since that first visit, the Orchestra has returned 11 times, and in November 2023, it returned to China to celebrate the 50th anniversary of its first visit. Terry added that an often-overlooked benefit of people-to-people exchanges is that they open up our horizons so we may see our own country in new and unexpected ways.

Terry's words struck a deep chord with me. Having spent most of my life living in the US, and a good part working in China, I sense intuitively that on every issue of importance, there are four underlying perspectives: how Americans view ourselves, how the Chinese view Americans, how the Chinese view themselves, and how Americans view the Chinese. Without understanding the four often competing and contradictory perspectives, and the historical and cultural reasons that gave rise to them, one cannot truly appreciate the vast differences and eerie similarities in how Americans and Chinese each think about our history, our government, our work, our relationships, our identities, and our destinies. The thoughtful adventurer may conclude in the end that "reality" is furthest from all four perspectives. In understanding and appreciating the different perspectives, however, the adventurer is made aware of what we share, what divides us, and what we can do to bridge the gap to create a common future. For example, is America the land of liberty and opportunity, leader of the free world, made better and stronger with each passing economic and political crisis? Or is it a superpower, once a model of emulation, now in irreversible decline? Is China, having lifted hundreds of millions out of poverty, becoming the land of opportunities and worthy of imitation? Or is China, authoritarian and foreign, incapable of global leadership, merely a richer and more powerful version of its flawed self?

Is government, as believed by many Americans, an intrinsic evil, that must be checked and balanced so that the true driver of society, individual initiative, will not be deterred? Or is government, as inculcated in China, an intrinsic good that watches over and provides for the people like a benevolent parent? Is relationship in America based on mutual affection and attraction? Or is it impulsive and self-centered? Is relationship in China premised on harmony and familial duties? Or is it too practical and calculated? Is America the land of freedom and personal liberty, full of rags to riches stories and the American dream? Or is America where the rich get richer and the poor get poorer? What is the American dream versus the Chinese dream? What does it mean to be American, a nation of immigrants; and to be Chinese, a nation once ancient and proud, now searching for a modern identity? I don't have answers to any of these questions. Yet I do know that our individual and collective search for a better society and a better world are enriched by exploring these and other conflicting perspectives, and in the process coming up with our own syntheses and conclusions.

The US and China together account for nearly 40% of global greenhouse gas emissions. Coordination between the two countries is essential for achieving meaningful reductions and combatting the effects of climate change. When one thinks of West Virigina, one typically thinks of coal country and coal miners hurt by the energy transition. Yet even here, people-to-people exchanges between the US and China have flourished. I spoke to Richard Bajura, Director Emeritus of the National Research Center for Coal and Energy, and formerly of the US–China Clean Energy Research Center (CERC) and Advanced Coal Technology Consortium. For over 10 years, he and his colleagues led efforts to develop and deploy advanced technologies that facilitate the energy transition, with public and private funding totaling over $250 million.

At its height, the US–China Clean Energy Research Center supported research for approximately 1,100 researchers in the US and China. According to an evaluation by the US Government Accountability Office, US participants gained "important benefits, such as the ability to speed progress in their research through cooperation with other US researchers and leading Chinese scientists and engineers and access to unique experimental platforms unavailable in the United States." To facilitate research and collaboration, CERC pioneered a novel Technology Management Plan that governed intellectual property developed under its purview. Within CERC, scientists who brought IP to CERC retained "all right, title, and interest in their background IP" and were not required to license, assign, or transfer it. The CERC Technology Management Plan asked, in the event of a dispute, that the parties reach a mutually agreeable resolution. If none could be reached, the Plan required submission of the dispute to arbitration under the rules of the United Nations Commission on International Trade Law. No instance of arbitration was ever reported under the CERC [26]. I asked Richard how the center came to existence in a state in which 90% of the electricity is generated by coal, and 50% of state revenue comes from coal. Richard disclosed that the center started when US–China government relations were good, and because it helped American researchers understand what their Chinese counterparts were doing and what worked and didn't work. For example, because the US has ample oil reserves, coal gasification has not been an important topic of research. On the other hand, China, short on oil reserves, has done important work in the area. Sharing of progress and obstacles helped Americans as much as they may help the Chinese. The center's charter expired during the Biden administration.

Based on the work of Autor, Dorn, and Hanson, we know that certain regions of America were disproportionately impacted by the China Shock. Yet even here, in the heartlands of America, people-to-people exchanges between the US and China blossom. Bob Holden served as Missouri's 53rd Governor from 2001 to 2005. After he retired from political office, he became President of the US Heartland China Association (USHCA), founded by the late Senator Adlai Stevenson and colleagues. USHCA covers 20 states that stretch from the Great Lakes to the Gulf of Mexico. Bob believes that expanded cultural ties and educational partnerships foster opportunities that lead to successes in both countries. Done well, American farmers can export more goods, American colleges can attract more talents, American companies can sell more products, and American students can learn more about Chinese culture and language. USHA hosts programs such as the Heartland Mayors Delegation to China to share city-to-city best practice around climate change, as well as the annual US–China Ag roundtable. Recent delegations included Mayor Jim Brainard of Carmel, Indiana; Mayor Barbara Buffaloe of Columbia, Missouri; Mayor Lee Harris of Shelby County, Tennessee; Mayor Chokwe Lumumba of Jackson, Mississippi; Mayor Kim Norton of Rochester, Minnesota; and Mayor Robyn Tannehill of Oxford, Mississippi. Their visit kicked off a Yangtze-Mississippi Municipality Energy Transition Exchange that enabled city-to-city best practice sharing around energy transition, climate mitigation, and green economy along these two major river communities [27].

Beyond profits, people-to-people exchanges can also save lives. In early 2020, the Committee of 100 raised $4 million from members and donors to combat COVID-19. Through our partnerships in China, we secured 850,000 N95 masks to send to 100 plus American hospitals and healthcare institutions in underserved communities. By partnering with the Association of Asian Pacific Community Health Organizations, Jewish Federations of North America, KAHAL, National Association for the Advancement of Colored People (NAACP), National Alliance for Hispanic Health, National Urban League, Partnership With Native Americans, US Heartland China Association, American Federation of Teachers, and Mayor's Fund to Advance New York City, the donations reached largely minority communities and the healthcare institutions that serve them. On other fronts, arts and culture have the ability to connect and transcend. On November 2022, the Committee of 100 and the Tianjin Juilliard School co-hosted a fireside chat on bridging cultures through music. Committee of 100 member and Tianjin Juilliard CEO and Artistic Director, Wei He and Dr. Joseph W. Polisi, President Emeritus and Chief China Officer at The Juilliard School, explored performing arts education in the US and China, Juilliard's journey in bridging cultures through music, and how arts education ties the global community [28]. During my tenure at Committee of 100, we launched US–China 2050, a thought leadership series that examines areas in which the US and China shared common interests. The first, "On Preventing a Devastating Pandemic," included Thomas R. Frieden, Former Director, US Centers for Disease Control and Prevention, George Fu Gao, Former Director-General, Chinese Center for Disease Control and Prevention, among others [29]. What the Committee of 100 does is not unique. Across the US, Americans are advancing exchanges and communications with the people of China, now more needed than ever before. Beyond people-to-people exchanges and communications, Americans can and should demand a more robust and open debate on our assumptions towards China, so that we may craft the best courses of action that protect our national security, secure our civil liberties, advance our economic interests, and avoid a sleepwalk into an armed conflict that puts all Americans at risk.

In January 2023, the Committee of 100 received an invitation to co-host the first ever Lunar New Year Celebration at Vice President Kamala Harris' official Washington D.C. residence. On January 31st, hundreds of Asian American political, business, and civic leaders gathered at the

Vice President's Residence to celebrate our common heritage and shared future. Before Vice President Harris came on, I had the honor to deliver a short message to the audience. In my remarks I uttered, "we are grateful to you and the President for both your sympathy and renewed commitment to policies that will reduce violence in our communities, especially gun violence and attacks directed against Asian Americans. We celebrate the Lunar New Year tonight—and the longer days and shorter nights to come." I have met President Biden and heard him speak on numerous occasions. I agree wholeheartedly when he says that America's best days are ahead of us. That every time anyone has counted us out, they have been proven wrong. Whether it be after the Revolutionary War when the newly created nation was facing runaway inflation and querulous states, or after the Civil War when the South lay in ruin and the country looked more divided than ever, or during the Great Depression when one out of every four working Americans was unemployed, every time America has been counted out, we have come back stronger and better.

I believe that this time is no different.

References

1. Council on Foreign Relations (2018) Excerpt: The Third Revolution. Available at: https://www.cfr.org/excerpt-third-revolution. Accessed 14 Aug 2025.
2. Voice of America (2016) Why Hasn't the US Signed the Law of the Sea Treaty? Available at: https://www.voanews.com/a/united-states-sign-law-sea-treaty/3364342.html. Accessed 14 Aug 2025.
3. Amnesty International (2023) Iraq: 20 years since the US-led coalition invaded Iraq, impunity reigns supreme. Available at: https://www.amnesty.org/en/latest/news/2023/03/iraq-20-years-since-the-us-led-coalition-invaded-iraq-impunity-reigns-supreme/. Accessed 14 Aug 2025.
4. U.S. Department of State (2023) GEC special report: How the People's Republic of China seeks to reshape the global information environment. Previously available at: https://www.state.gov/gec-special-report-how-the-peoples-republic-of-china-seeks-to-reshape-the-global-information-environment/. Accessed 14 Aug 2025.
5. Committee of 100 (2023) Diplomatic language guide memo. Available at: https://www.committee100.org/committee-of-100-diplomatic-language-guide-memo/. Accessed 14 Aug 2025.

6. Politico (2022) Tough on China gains traction as electoral test. Available at: https://www.politico.com/newsletters/politico-china-watcher/2022/02/10/tough-on-china-gains-traction-as-electoral-test-00007570. Accessed 14 Aug 2025.
7. Gallup (2021) New high in perceptions of China as U.S.'s greatest enemy. Available at: https://news.gallup.com/poll/337457/new-high-perceptions-china-greatest-enemy.aspx. Accessed 14 Aug 2025.
8. National Park Service (2023) Vincent Chin. Available at: https://www.nps.gov/people/vincent-chin.htm. Accessed 14 Aug 2025.
9. InsideEVs (2024) 'The Most Humbling Thing I've Ever Seen': Ford CEO On China's Car Industry. Available at: https://insideevs.com/news/764318/ford-ceo-china-evs-humbled/. Accessed 14 Aug 2025.
10. New York Times (2025) Trump Will Slow, but May Not Stop, the Rise of Electric Vehicles. Available at: https://www.nytimes.com/2025/08/03/business/trump-electric-vehicles.html. Accessed 14 Aug 2025.
11. Wall Street Journal (2025) GM Will Import EV Batteries From China's CATL Despite Tariffs. Available at: https://www.wsj.com/business/autos/gm-bolt-china-ev-batteries-1562e2f7. Accessed 14 Aug 2025.
12. Wall Street Journal (2024) How China is churning out EVs faster than everyone else. Available at: https://www.wsj.com/business/autos/how-china-is-churning-out-evs-faster-than-everyone-else-df316c71. Accessed 14 Aug 2025.
13. Quality Assurance Magazine (2022) New study reveals most popular cuisines in America. Available at: https://www.qualityassurancemag.com/news/new-study-reveals-most-popular-cuisines-in-america/. Accessed 14 Aug 2025.
14. University of North Georgia (n.d.) Chinese Flagship Program. Available at: https://ung.edu/modern-languages/chinese-flagship/index.php. Accessed 14 Aug 2025.
15. U.S. Department of State (n.d.) 100,000 Strong Educational Exchange Initiatives. Available at: https://2009-2017.state.gov/100k/index.htm. Accessed 14 Aug 2025.
16. NBC News (2023) How the U.S.-China clash is being felt on campus. Available at: https://www.nbcnews.com/news/world/americans-study-china-university-tensions-rcna87203. Accessed 14 Aug 2025.
17. Larsen R (2023) Larsen, Beyer and Chu Reintroduce Legislation to Restore Fulbright Exchanges with China. Available at: https://larsen.house.gov/news/documentsingle.aspx?DocumentID=2741. Accessed 14 Aug 2025.
18. U.S. Congress (2022) H.R.8939—Restoring Fulbright Exchanges with China and Hong Kong Act. Available at: https://www.congress.gov/bill/117th-congress/house-bill/8939/text. Accessed 14 Aug 2025.

19. Halberstam D (1972) The Best and the Brightest. Random House, New York
20. John F. Kennedy Presidential Library and Museum (1963) Commencement address at American University. Available at: https://www.jfklibrary.org/archives/other-resources/john-f-kennedy-speeches/american-university-19630610. Accessed 14 Aug 2025.
21. Council on Foreign Relations (2022) The Chinese Communist Party. Available at: https://www.cfr.org/backgrounder/chinese-communist-party. Accessed 14 Aug 2025.
22. Britannica (n.d.) Chinese Communist Party. Available at: https://www.britannica.com/topic/Chinese-Communist-Party. Accessed 14 Aug 2025.
23. NBC News (2022) China eases restrictions in major move away from 'zero-Covid' after protests. Available at: https://www.nbcnews.com/news/world/china-eases-restrictions-zero-covid-protests-rcna60479. Accessed 14 Aug 2025.
24. U.S. Department of State (2021) Ping Pong Diplomacy: Historic 1971 U.S. table tennis trip to China. Available at: https://diplomacy.state.gov/ping-pong-diplomacy-historic-1971-u-s-table-tennis-trip-to-china/. Accessed 14 Aug 2025.
25. New York Times (2002) John Kamm's third way. Available at: https://www.nytimes.com/2002/03/03/magazine/john-kamm-s-third-way.html. Accessed 14 Aug 2025.
26. Wikipedia (n.d.) U.S.–China Clean Energy Research Center. Available at: https://en.wikipedia.org/wiki/US%E2%80%93China_Clean_Energy_Research_Center. Accessed 14 Aug 2025.
27. U.S. Heartland China Association (2023) U.S. Heartland mayors bridge the Mississippi and Yangtze communities with historic China visit. Available at: https://usheartlandchina.org/press-release/u-s-heartland-mayors-bridge-the-mississippi-and-yangtze-communities-with-historic-china-visit/. Accessed 14 Aug 2025.
28. Committee of 100 (2022) Bridging cultures through music. Available at: https://www.committee100.org/blog/event-takeaways-bridging-cultures-through-music/. Accessed 14 Aug 2025.
29. Committee of 100 (2023) U.S.–China 2050: Preventing a devastating pandemic. Available at: https://www.committee100.org/upcoming-event/us-china-2050-preventing-a-devastating-pandemic/. Accessed 14 Aug 2025.

Index

Z. Z. Huang, *Rethinking China*,
https://doi.org/10.1007/978-981-95-3608-5

9789819536078